# THE
# CREEPING
# HOURS
# OF TIME

BY THE SAME AUTHOR

*Via Ypres (A Record of the Field
Ambulances, 39 Div. B.E.F.)*
Suffolk Yesterdays
This Suffolk
North-east Suffolk
Household and Country Crafts
An Hour-glass on the Run
A Window in Suffolk
Under a Suffolk Sky
A Suffolk Calendar
In Suffolk Borders
The Felixstowe Story
Suffolk Remembered
Suffolk Villages
Victorian Suffolk
Portrait of Suffolk
Suffolk Miscellany

# THE CREEPING HOURS OF TIME

an autobiography by
ALLAN JOBSON

ROBERT HALE · LONDON

ISBN 0 7091 5956 0

Robert Hale Limited
Clerkenwell House
45–47 Clerkenwell Green
London EC1

PRINTED IN GREAT BRITAIN BY
CLARKE, DOBLE & BRENDON LTD
PLYMOUTH

# Contents

# Illustrations

FOR MY FAMILY
AND ALL MY SUFFOLK FRIENDS

It is rather significant of the march of time that the street cries and little unattributed quotations in these pages, the lingua franca of our childhood, have passed into folklore. So be it. They have been classified by the student, yet remain as bees in amber.

# Introduction

For a child, one of the great sights of London suburban streets of yesterday was a steam-roller. Ours was just splendid, with a horse rampant in brass on the front of its boiler and a fly-wheel that spun like a top. I do not think I am romancing or that I dreamt it, although I may have done, but I seem to remember a man with a red flag walking in front of it because the speed limit then was five miles an hour and the law said that care had to be taken. Cyclists in those days, who wore caps and knickerbockers like overgrown schoolboys, were a very venturesome breed, and looked like it, taking a childish delight in breaking the law and being fined for speeding. It seems incredible, therefore, that one lifetime should span the years to culminate in a meteoric marvel such as Concorde, faster than sound, which is taken for granted and even described as a stinking, noisy nuisance.

We have moved a good deal faster than a steam-roller, and life has lost something of its magic. No longer does a boy have to save up his pennies to buy an eggbox to make himself a rabbit hutch, or a girl beg for a pin to see a peep show. But we had our moments—"To make some special instant special blest". Especially when the Brighton fast greased by, a real throbbing engine, and we watched how our Anerley bridge cut the smoke in two!

One of the turning points in my life came when I learnt to read. I remember sitting on the floor of my father's workshop, back to the wall, when the miracle happened, and the instrument was a penny book for the bairns. Alas, my pennies were so few and my appetite large. The next step was to read a book all through, which in my case was *Swiss Family Robinson*. This was a tiny volume in blinding print, but I closed the book and told my father of my accomplishment. Life was never the same again, it had suddenly become larger.

In those days people used to speculate as to what would happen when all the coal was used up, and other similar trifles. If I had any such irksome thoughts, I would just snuggle down in bed and listen to the shunting of the coal trucks that almost came up to my bedroom window, rattled against the buffers and were left until the morning; and people with twelve chimneys had twelve fires as Mary McCarthy has reminded us.

It is true our streets were a bit drab, but even so there was a bluebell wood not far away, and my father and I could wander where the birds sang, where the chestnuts lit their candles, the laburnum dropped its gold and the lilac—"Those flowers made of light"—grew by the way.

In my mother's home county of Suffolk old country methods and ways of life were coming to an end.

The great old kingdoms have gone, including our Empire:

> But the dreams their children dreamed,
>   Fleeting, unsubstantial, vain,
> Shadowy as the shadows seemed,
> Airy nothing, as they deemed,
>   These remain.
>
> MARY  COLERIDGE

# 1
# The World of Innocence

His best companion innocence and health;
And his best riches, ignorance of wealth.
OLIVER GOLDSMITH

I was born in the sunset years of Queen Victoria's reign, a truly wonderful era in which to enter life with its marked sense of security, completeness and finality. It fostered a comfortable feeling in a child basking in such an atmosphere which penetrated even to a poor home. One was too young to question the enigma of extreme poverty which existed cheek by jowl with such inordinate prosperity. A horse-drawn carriage ushered in that long and significant reign, but an internal combustion engine spluttered it out. The era began in simplicity with its face to the past and the advantages won at Trafalgar and Waterloo, but ended in complexity and a dread of the future.

It has been said that thrift, patriotism and religion were the outstanding virtues of that era. Certainly those qualities were very prominent, not only in our home but in the neighbourhood ruled over by a vestry.

Our mother was a countrywoman out of a Suffolk village, a neat, capable, spruce little woman with long dark hair, hazel eyes, a kindly heart and a great capacity for making ends meet. As a household it would have been nothing if not controlled by the thrift exercised by her, because Father with all his strivings only earned a few shillings a week and never more than twenty-five to thirty shillings. But we were respectable on that, with a best suit for Sunday.

13

Father was born in Lincoln in 1850, the illegitimate son of a so-called surgeon, Edward Jacklin Mason, whose father in turn was a surgeon in High Street. This was a stigma that shadowed my father all his life. He had rather plaintive blue eyes, a large nose in the Caborn family tradition, and was greatly interested in birds. When a thunderstorm loomed he would climb up to the top of our house to watch the lightning. He wore a beard all his life and was fastidious about his hands. As far as I was concerned he could cut out paper animals that would really stand up.

When Mother left her Suffolk village of necessity because her father was but a farm labourer, she went from one lovely spot to another. How she got from Devonshire Street, Shoreditch to The Lions, Fox Hill, Upper Norwood I would not know, neither do I know how lonely she felt. I do not suppose there was any-one to meet her or show her the way across London, but she had that sturdy independence that a long line of country an-cestors had bequeathed to her. Her very name was of the county and one branch of the family had been armigerous. In other words she was of stout yeoman stock.

The red-brick villa, guarded by two Coade-stone lions, (hence its name 'The Lions'), was at the bottom of a very steep hill which had been channelled out from a sandy scrubby eminence that gave a fine view into the Weald of Kent. It was an ideal spot, where birds sang and flowers could be had for the search-ing. Indeed, it was still the country, so lately had it been urban-ized. Did Mother pine for her old home? I do not think so; indeed she was a forerunner, being followed in turn by her two sisters.

Upper Norwood was indeed a lovely spot. Those old planners could not find names suggestive enough for the locality. Fox Hill led into Church Road and at the southern end was All Saints' Church surrounded by a tumbled acre enclosed by iron railings. Adjacent was the village school, recalling the influence for good the Church then had on the rising generation. The incumbent lived in a very nice house in the road with a long garden behind a wall that skirted Sylvan Hill. Then there was Beulah Hill with its spa down the side of which in a rural retreat lived Spurgeon, the great preacher. There was Gipsy Hill where the Gipsy Queen had held sway, Jasper Hill, Belvedere Road (where my wife and I were destined to start housekeeping) and Auckland Road lined by large houses and still larger gardens that required more than one gardener apiece.

Mother was deeply religious and that was her safeguard because she was soon linked up with chapel folk of Wesleyan Methodism in a building at the top of Gipsy Hill; and it was there she met our father. I do not think she was at The Lions very long because she found a place in Beulah Hill. The lady of the house, whether spinster or widow I cannot tell, caught Mother in the act of making her wedding cake. Again, I am not sure of the consequences. What I do know is that Father had taken a job as a journeyman shoemaker, or repairer with a Methodist family in the Anerley Road and it was in their house that my parents lodged in rooms. So evidently between the wedding cake and the wedding she had left Beulah Hill.

The courtship could not have been of long duration. True, Mother had taken Father home to be vetted by her own folk but it lasted long enough for the Methodist cause to have grown out of the chapel at Gipsy Hill into a pretentious church of the neo-Gothic style in Westow Hill in 1876. They were the first couple to be married there, Mother being twenty-three and Father twenty-six. The Bible that was given them perished in the blitz.

Mother certainly had her share of trouble, yet she was the pivot around which our family life revolved. She dominated the scene, for without her we could do nothing. She did this not in a self-assertive manner but as the natural order of things. She became a most anxious parent, far too anxious and possessive for my liking since I was the last of four children; but it may have been occasioned by the loss of the middle two, a boy and a girl. On their birthdays I was given a penny, something which came my way very infrequently. But what a wretched penny it was, a morbid melancholy coin watered with tears. If I should complain of feeling unwell (I never did unless forced), it was a dose of castor oil and a visit from the doctor. Oh, that oil! I think Baring Gould sums up the fear and the dread of it when writing about the old corner cupboard and the castor-oil spoon.

Then when I was a very little boy Father went down with pneumonia. Those must have been dreadful days for a poor woman without an income. However, he survived, although he was left with a chronic dry cough. I think it was all this trouble that made our poverty so pressing and sent Mother out charring. I remember her going to a lovely house set well back inside the gravelled drive in the leafy part of Sydenham. I must have been very small but I can remember going with my father in the evenings to meet her, waiting discreetly out of sight for her to appear from the side of the drive. Sometimes she would bring home a parcel which on investigation showed the parts of an ox that never otherwise crossed our threshold. How lovely and succulent those crumbs from a rich man's table were. At another period she did the chores at the famous Anerley Bicycling Club which was in premises in the Ridsdale Road, just round the corner from our street. But this work had to be abandoned because of her health.

What was the matter I cannot tell but it meant an operation in Great Ormond Street Hospital and melancholy visits by my Father and myself on a Sunday. I remember her flushed face as she lay in bed and the fear that she would die. It cast a great gloom over our household. However, she lived to come home again and considered it was her homoeopathic doctor and treatment that saved her life. (I notice a book has been published on the ancient art describing it as being an ever-growing force in medicine today). For a long period she had to rest at home and Father would read to her one of the *Sunday at Home* serials, such as "Mrs Haliburton's Troubles".

Unfortunately Mother's religious outlook, which to her was such a joy, became almost horrific as the years passed and as far as we were concerned. Father took his religion more gently as befitted his temperament.

My brother was eleven years older than me and I can just remember him going to school for the last time, but only that and no other occasion. He was a good scholar and went in for the essay competition of the RSPCA, winning it first time. He was hoping to receive the prize from the hands of Princess Christian at the Crystal Palace but it was the Baroness Burdett Coutts instead. He managed to get a clerkship in the City and sometimes would bring home a penny toy bought from the kerbside vendors on London Bridge.

When Father was taken ill it was the local doctor who attended him. Why Mother changed over to homoeopathy I cannot tell. The new doctor came from Sydenham and paid his visits on foot. I remember his stick stethoscope which he kept in his coat-tail pocket, his pince-nez fastened to his coat by thin gold wire with a tiny gold ball or two at the joints, his gold watch and particularly his doomlike, "Ahs!" His fee was two and sixpence a visit but I think he repaid it by cast-off clothes belonging to his two sons, or a bonnet for Mother that had graced his very ladylike wife. He would stop for a little chat tell us about his sons at Oxford of whom he was very proud and how when he lost a little boy he opened the window to let out the spirit as death took place. If he could not come he would send a neighbour, a Dr Shackleton, who was the father of Sir Ernest. When Mother wore the bonnet at chapel it caused a few glances in her direction.

As a child when I had to be washed before bed and Father had to do the job, I did not appreciate his gentle touch, much preferring Mother's more business-like approach. Sometimes on a Sunday evening when Mother had gone to the service and I was left alone with him he would talk about his mother, how she played the organ at Ewhurst Church and how he did a bit of bell ringing. He even knew about windmills and how they had to get up in the night to reef the sails; but he would never speak of his father.

It was natural that Father should take his mother's name but a little curious that his father's name was added, so he became Edward Mason Jobson. His line of Jobson's came from Horncastle; they were cattle graziers and connected with ship-owners at Spurn Point. Why Mason did not marry Grandmother I cannot tell, but she was only a girl when her mother died. In any case Mason himself was dead at thirty.

Father's early years were spent with his grandfather and his mother at 7 Monson Street, Lincoln. As he grew up he must have spent much of his time in the open air because he learned at an early age to fish in the Witham and in true boylike fashion fell in. He was saved from drowning by a dog, so the tale goes. Then, jumping off a heap of stones with other boys, he dislocated his kneecap. He was taken home, placed on the kitchen table, his knee was hacked about without anaesthetics and he was lamed for life.

The grandfather was a very kind man who must have been fond of his little waif. He wrote to Father until the end of his long life and Father kept his letters. They usually enclosed little gifts of money and of course good advice.

Father's grandmother must have been a very attractive person. She was Elizabeth Caborn born at Beverley, Yorkshire in 1786, her name being derived from the village near Caistor in Lincolnshire, the place of her ancestors. Her childhood was spent at Beverley where she was noticed by the wife of the colonel of the county militia who was a nobleman. When the regiment left the town the lady begged that Bessy might go with her. In this novel situation she saw much of life, travelling over most of England, Scotland and Ireland in the most stirring times.

She had a good many admirers but she chose a soldier, rather against her father's wishes. On 7th September 1809 she was married to John Jobson at Dovercourt parish church, where the North Lincolnshire militia was then stationed. They had a large family, sixteen children, most of whom died young. One little boy was killed by the trunk of a tree rolling on him in a local coachmaker's yard. They were all buried in St Mark's Church-yard, Lincoln, beside their grandfather Caborn. Elizabeth died in 1840 and was also buried there.

We might now turn to the 1841 Census which was the first made in Victoria's reign and the first that gave names instead of numbers. The relevant entry runs: "172 High Street, Lincoln, in the parish of St Mary le Wigford. John Jobson, 53, Straw hat maker, Mary Jobson, 15, Hannah Jobson, 15, Eliza Jobson, 8, Sarah Caborn, 50, bonnet maker." The latter was a sister-in-law and aunt to the children.

The 1851 Census gives the address as 7 Monson Street and the occupants John Jobson, 63, Hannah Jobson, 25, Edward Mason Jobson, 11 months, (my father) and Sarah Caborn, 61.

Father was given a good education and taught to write a quite distinguished hand. Later his mother had married a John Spencer Wardale and moved to the Guildford area taking Father with her. One of his enjoyments there was to wander in Farn-ham Castle Park. One day he managed to capture a small fawn. He hurried off home with such a lovely find and was surprised when it caused great consternation and was hurriedly returned to where it belonged, probably after nightfall. His mother died aged forty-three at Pound Lane, Godalming in 1868. In 1865 by reason of his lameness he had been apprenticed to a cord-wainer for seven long years. During this period and by reason of his education he kept his master's books.

A few of grandmother's letters were preserved by Father. These contain little human touches showing how she hoped he would be able to get home and how pleased the girls would be (his two step-sisters). "Mary Ann is eight years old next Mon-day. They often talk about you and reckon very much of seeing you. Do you think you could bring me a few plants, for the frost has killed every one of mine. I should very much like a scented geranium like the other if I could get one." Then: "Godalming, June 5/68, Dear Edward, Your grandfather came last night, if you could possibly get over again to spend Sunday with us he would be very pleased. He may go back in a few days, we cannot tell. Make yourself as nice as you can, I fear there will not be time for you to get your crutch painted." Father kept these letters locked in his box beside his bench and they were not seen by prying eyes until after his death.

The Jobson line is not without interest, spreading right across the Midlands. There are three in the *Dictionary of National Biography*. Taken in chronological order the first is Sir Francis Jobson, died 1573, lieutenant of the Tower. He connected himself with the Dudley family through his marriage with Elizabeth Plantagenet, third daughter and co-heiress of Arthur, Viscount Lisle, natural son of Edward IV. He ended up at Monkwich and was buried in the Church of St Giles, Colchester.

Next comes Richard Jobson, traveller, who was appointed in 1620 to command an expedition to explore the River Gambia in the interests of "the gentlemen adventurers for the countries of Guinea and Benin". It is recorded that he did not meet with the gold which was the principal object in view. He kept a journal which was published, an extract from which is of interest: "They have great store of Locust Trees and Wild Honey: the Cola is like our bigger sort of chestnut; flat on both sides, yet without a hard shell, the taste is very bitter, yet causes that which is taken after it to taste very sweet; for so I found it made Water taste like White-wine and Sugar: 50 of these will buy a Wife. They have a sensitive Plant, like our great Bramble-Bush on the River's Bank."

The third is Frederick James Jobson, D.D. (1812–1881) my father's uncle and first child of John and Elizabeth. After being apprenticed to E. J. Willson, a distinguished architect of Lincoln and having an art training from William Hilton, Keeper of the Royal Academy, he entered the Methodist ministry. He married his cousin Elizabeth Caborn but had no issue. He went as a representative to America and insisted on preaching to the negroes. Then with his wife he was sent on a deputation to Australia. He became Book Steward for the Methodist Society at very short notice, a post which he greatly developed and was President of the Methodist Conference in 1869. One of his early achievements was *Chapel and School Architecture*, 1850, which acted as a guide book when Methodism was developing fast, building churches, chapels and schools. He is buried in Highgate Cemetery, very near to George Eliot who in her writings shows a profound knowledge of Methodism.

He took a watchful interest in my father, sending him a five-pound note twice a year, which meant so much in those days. When he died at Highbury Place of overwork and insomnia, to both of which the Victorians were prone, his widow carried on the good work. She moved to Highbury Hill and Father was not to make an appearance unless asked to do so. If he was in her good books he was addressed as "Dear Edward", but if not it was "Dear Mr Jobson". When she died Father benefited in the will by £500 and we had some of the lovely treasures that had made up their home, because besides other accomplishments F. J. Jobson was an artist. Naturally these relations constituted a sort of lodestar in our lives. Before I was born Mrs Jobson paid a visit of inspection to our home to see Mother but was evidently satisfied.

Another member of the clan has just come to light, a Samuel Jobson who died in March 1687. He left his cottage and land at Brantigham, Yorkshire to his wife and on her death to the churchwardens of South Cave. A condition was that on every Easter Tuesday a specific sermon should be preached and afterwards bread to the value of twenty shillings given to the poor. A new scheme was approved by the Charity Commissioners in 1883 when the land was sold whereby the vicar of South Cove receives fifteen pounds towards his stipend, a third for the repair of the parish church and the remainder to the "needs of the necessitous residents of the parish". The small oval-shaped loaves are still baked by a member of the parish and were distributed this year (1975).

I was extremely interested by *The Life of Thomas Cooper* (1805–92), written by himself, published in 1872 and described as one of the best autobiographies of Victorian times. He was a Chartist and went to prison. He states: "My mother's race bore the old Saxon name of Jobson and were small farmers and carriers in Lincolnshire; and some of them fishermen on the sea coast. . . .

"In the autumn season two or three weeks of gleaning holidays were spent at Market Rasen with my uncle Luke Jobson, my mother's brother. He rented some twenty-four acres of land under Squire Tennyson of Tealby; and also followed the occupation of a weekly carrier, as did his father, Luke Jobson before him—his father, Luke Jobson, whose father Henry Jobson, was an innkeeper at Northampton. I can go no higher with my genealogy on the maternal side. . . .

"The ride in the carrier's cart, too, between Rasen and Gainsborough had its delights. One time we set off from Rasen late at night and drew up in an open field sometime before the morning broke to let the horse graze a little. I have the most lively recollection of awakening in the cart and looking in amazement at what seemed to be hundreds of small, dull, strange-looking lights, scattered over a wide field. My uncle told me they were glow worms and he had never seen so many together before. Nor have I ever had such a vision of wonder as that since boyhood.

"Each Friday in the week—the day that Uncle came to Gainsborough as weekly carrier—I was closely attendant upon him when school hours were over, having to read the directions on his letters and parcels, for he was never put to school; and to his dying day 'Knew never a litter i' th' book, save a round O,' as he used to say. . . .

"And when I first saw one of the pictures of Gainsborough

I thought he must have felt in the woods of Suffolk similar raptures to that which I felt in the woods of old Lincolnshire."

Cooper well knew F. J. Jobson, who next to his wife was the most valuable friend of his life; the autobiography is dedicated to him, although he did not claim any relationship.

It suffices to state that the only Northamptonshire token was issued by a George Jobson, banker, in 1794 and on the reverse is: "May Northamptonshire flourish, $\frac{1}{2}$d".

# 2

# Down Our Street

---

Cold's the wind, and wet's the rain,
Saint Hugh be our good speed:
Ill is the weather that bringeth no gain,
Nor helps good hearts in need.

THOMAS DEKKER

Mother's first child, a son, was not born at number 6 Anerley Road, but at her old home in Suffolk, or at least where her father and mother then lived. In due time, probably soon after his birth, a new home was made in a new little terrace house in a road backing on to Anerley station on the old London, Brighton and South Coast Railway. Curiously enough it was named after St Hugh, a saint whose patronage sheds an aura about the cathedral set on a hill, under whose towers my father was born. But that was the only claim to saintliness the street possessed, because there was only one other road that vied with it for notoriety and squalor. Yet it was a by-way which lives in the memory by reason of the life that was lived in it.

At the top was a huge gin palace that was responsible for the street's character, and at the other end a little mission church. I can still hear faintly the little bell which called us on a Sabbath evening, either to hear the curate preach, who might have been the genial young Taylor Smith who was to become the Chaplain General in the First World War, or more probably the soft-voiced stipendary lay reader, both of whom would come to see Mother on pastoral visits. As for the 'Anerley Arms', that needed no bell. The flashy lights were enough.

though the doors closed with a noise we could hear in our half-basement living-room.

But there was one touch about that pub which was a sheer delight, occasioned when they replenished the cellars. Up would come a brewer's dray, pulled by two or four spanking horses probably Suffolks. The men would get down, take off their hard-hats and replace them with red stockinged caps, the very same as worn by Nelson's sailors of the Line, but which were also the traditional head-gear of the maltsters, as used at the maltings when the barley arrived on the farm wagons. They would don their aprons, put the nosebags on the horses, parbuckle the barrels into the cellars, and when all was done leave behind chaff and droppings that provided the sparrows with a perfect feast. We could see all this from our windows as the cellar opening was actually in our street.

St Hugh's Road was on an incline and it throbbed with humanity. During the day there would be all sorts of callers whose voices needed no aids to make themselves heard. The greengrocer sold everything in season: peas, beans, potatoes, cabbages, apples, pears, strawberries, cherries, gooseberries and currants. Mother could make the most delicious mixed-fruit puddings boiled in a basin. Then there was the fish merchant, wheeling his "all fresh" load on a costermonger's barrow. After all we were not a long way from Billingsgate. We might have had a few shrimps if the money ran to it, but wet fish, winkles and shellfish in general were taboo, as Mother was sceptical as to whether they were stored under his bed. She seemed to have an allergy about under-the-bed storage. Then there was the coalman, so that one could buy a sack at a time when needed. Mother, being thrifty, used to get in a stock in the summer, the best she could buy. I recall the genial old man who used to deliver through the front door, going along our passage and down a flight of rickety stairs to an anchorage under the stairs. I have often wondered how he did it, without a word of complaint, in two-hundredweight bags.

The milk was delivered very early in small metal cans with brass fittings, and the milkman would even make a second call during the day. This milkfloat was like a Roman chariot with bells on the horses, though some milkmen had simply a churn set in a perambulator. The baker made his rounds with a huge basket, possibly two, one on each arm, or by a barrow. We used to fetch our bread from the shop and thus get the extra bit known as the make-weight. What I remember of it, the bread was lovely, especially the Nevill's bread, which I think was made partly with milk.

The dustman came once a week. The cart was a tumbrel with a small ladder attached that could be placed in position at the side. The dustbin was a brick affair in our tiny back garden, so that the man would go down the stairs with a large basket, shovel out the refuse, mount the stairs and climb the ladder to shoot the stuff into the hopper-top of the cart. True there was a cloud of dust, but we were used to that, particularly when the wind blew and took off the surface of the road. I think something was said about everyone having to eat a peck of dust, which brings me to our sanitation. Our road was paved and channelled but in common with even the best thoroughfares, owing to horse transport there was a good supply of horse droppings. This did not create much of a problem because there were amongst the sober and provident a good many gardeners. They were glad of a few pails of this excellent manure, freely bestowed. Besides, boys were not above hawking it about for a penny a pailful.

Every now and again the drains were emptied. Men with long-handled scoops would come, ladle out the mud and leave the pats for a cart which followed to take them away. The work was not synchronized, so that small children had a splendid chance to enjoy themselves. It is hardly to be wondered that epidemics occurred, such as small-pox, scarlet fever and diphtheria. This led to the appearance of the fever van, to me a dreadful affair. I can see it now. It was a closed one-horse van, with a driver and a porter, both wearing peaked caps. I used to think they looked like emissaries of the devil. The first visit was for the hapless patient and a second call for the bedding. Thank God they never came for me.

Being a crowded street, there were two pathetic touches, all too frequent. One was the passage of the little white coffins, and the other the pauper funeral. The latter consisted of a decrepit old carriage with storage space under the driving seat, covered with a bedraggled hammer-cloth. Into this the poor old coffin was pushed. It might well have called forth the saw:

> Rattle his bones over the stones,
> He's only a pauper whom nobody owns.

I shouldn't think any of those poor old bodies were ever taken into one of our local churches. These events saw a weekly pilgrimage on a Sunday afternoon, when families, draped in black carrying flowers, made their way to our local cemetery, which was at Elmers End next to a sewage farm, the smell of which I associated with the decomposition of the bodies.

But we had happier visitors such as those who sold pot plants, all a blowin' and a growin', although they were alleged to have been stolen. Or caged birds that might prove to be no songsters because:

> We found some old cock-sparrow's feathers
> A comin' thro' the dye.

The most melodious of all were those selling lavender, because the lavender fields of Mitcham were not far away. What lovely voices they had:

> Will you buy my sweet blooming lavender?
> There's your sixteen dark blue branches a penny, all in full
>     bloom.
> You buy it once, you will buy it twice;
> It will make your linen clothes smell sweet and nice.
> Come all you young ladies and make no delay
> I gathered my sweet lavender and am round once a day.

This was sung with the left hand cupped below the cheek to give the echo. At that time the girls and young women in our street would hardly have been called *ladies*.

Neither must I omit the cats' meat man, with his skewers of old horse. The old cats knew him and came running along, dogs or no dogs.

And there was the vendor of salt, his crystal load carried on a coster's barrow and covered over with old sacks, lest presumably it should rain. He seemed to have a two-way neck in case he should miss somebody who wanted a pennorth. He had a counterpart, a soft sibilant enquirer who wondered whether you required any arthstone, ma'am? Those old family hearths around which we gathered needed hearthstoning to make them white, and also blackleading with special brushes. Hearthstone was also in great demand for those long flights of steps which led to the front door.

There were others and they all seemed to bear the burden of a song, which extended even to the rag and bone man. The grimy and drab remains of an upholstered fashion caused him to sing. He sought the faded splendours of wool and silk, together with bones and old iron. His full-throated voice with bell accompaniment was rich in melody; and he would even pay in coppers for ridding you of a noisome pestilence. I suppose two wars and an intensified course in salvage have put an end to his activities.

Among these dealers was a colourful example who was known as Bob Plumb. He stood six feet two in his socks, wore a frock coat and top hat, drove a shaggy pony that was never groomed, while seated in a small cart. The pony would snap at all and sundry as they passed by, while Bob sang a rising scale— "bo-ooNEs!" It was said he had seen better days, which may have been the case. If so then he could have shaken hands with a rubicund tenor who sang extracts from operas to a harp played by an accompanist. He wore a buttonhole and winked at the errand boys.

The fly-paper man was another. His sign was a tall hat decorated with sticky papers. He would sing of their ability to "Catch 'em alive, O". After all he did a useful job because we had flies in plenty because of the horse droppings.

But I have forgotten the vendors of ice cream and,

> Hokey-pokey, penny a lump!
> The more you eat the more you jump!

The companion piece in winter to the ice-cream barrow was in the tin galley of the baked chestnut or hot-potato merchant who spread a little warmth and glow outside our pub.

Another gaily painted, nicely shaped cart, adorned with gold letters, was that of the sarsaparilla tincture, presided over by a gentleman wearing a fawn top hat. But that was for the dyspeptic grown-up and not seen in our street.

There was also that elfin-like load, borne aloft on a board covered over with a white cloth and another of green baize and heralded by a handbell. The tinkle could be heard in the distance coming nearer and nearer on dark evenings. This was the muffin man. Every now and then there would be a silence and one knew he had been stopped, his load would be lowered and a pile of doughy discs transferred to a plate; and the bell would sound again.

Besides all these vendors who sought a livelihood, there were the nondescript band who sought alms. Why they should choose our poor street was a mystery, but presumably they believed that the poor might help the poor. They ranged from the pathetic column who declared

> We don't want to shirk
> Any kind of hard work,
> But, kind friends, we can't get it to do,

to individual street singers who moved along slowly with an ear on the shoulder (as the Arabs say, meaning keeping alert) for the odd coin. A well-known hymn produced the best results. A window might open, a coin be heard to drop, a pause in the song and "Thank you, kind lady," as the copper was retrieved lest it rolled into the drain.

There was also instrumental music such as a barrel or piano organ, even the rare hurdy-gurdy, the latter with perhaps a monkey. Poor old trio, the player out from Tuscany with soft melting eyes and tattered clothes, the monkey irritated by fleas as well as tormenting children; and the wheezy instrument on its stump. Indeed it was known as the beggar's lyre.

> With dead, dull, doleful, heavy hums,
> With mournful moans, with grievous groans,
> The sober hurdy-gurdy thrums.

Some had but a tin whistle which they could play finely, or maybe a flute, concertina, piccolo or trumpet. Occasionally it was a bagpiper in a kilt whose weird strains always fascinated me. If a brass-band, the players would be Germans.

There was another most picturesque caller, the scissor-grinder or travelling tinker. He came with his wonderfully decorated perambulator, with its brass bands and balls all aglow, and his swinging fire, particularly his fire, into which was thrust his soldering iron. He too had a song:

> Have you any knives to grind?
> Carving knives or other knives to grind?
> Have you any chairs to mend?
> Or other things to mend?

Sometimes his bedraggled woman would come with him, and between them they would repair doormats and recane old chairs, working in the gutter. But the hairy, grimy husband was at his best grinding a knife and making the sparks fly.

Our street was at its most memorable in the long days when it seemed full of playing children. Opposite our house was a lamp-post offering a splendid stance not only for cricket, played with a home-made bat and ball, until a window was broken, when the game was abandoned *sine die*; but as a hold for a skipping-rope which would stretch right across the road:

> Black currant, red currant, raspberry tart
> Tell me the name of your sweet heart.

Or, more in keeping with the character of our street,

> Half a pint of Porter,
> A penny on the can,
> Hop there and back again
> IF YOU CAN.

And I can remember seeing a boy with a grotto. This was a picturesque little affair out of some distant past. A few bricks would be placed near a wall or fence on which were cockle or escallop shells garnished with grass or leaves. A few candle ends lighted up the little shrine:

> Please to remember the Grotter,
>   Only once a year.
> Father's gone to sea, Mother's gone to fetch him home,
>   Please remember me!

On the opposite corner to the public house was a little green-grocer's-cum-sweet shop, a rather grimy affair but I believe the man came from Mother's county. The backyard of this ran down by the pathway and was walled in by a smooth-cemented and painted wall. This gave a fine surface for several games. There was, for instance, a splendid bouncing ball game played with a button. The latter was placed a certain distance from the wall and one had to throw the ball a glancing bounce to hit the button and thence to the wall, catching the ball on the rebound. The time came when no further bounces could be made. I am not sure if the bounces were counted and he who made the fewest won the game. Incidentally, we collected buttons-brassies, tinnies and boneys. Then too, buttons were used as counters, tossed on to or beyond a line chalked on the path parallel to the wall. Cigarette cards were also used, flicking them on to or beyond the line; sometimes a cap was used.

Next to this shop was a fried fish shop where they used dripping. My word, how it stank! Then came a rather nice little grocer's, and next was a newly built sorting office of H.M. Post Office. To this came once or twice a day the Royal Mail van drawn by fast-running ponies and driven by experienced drivers in fine style. It was not difficult to imagine oneself back in the stage-coach era as they climbed over our railway bridge.

Our letters came direct from this office, delivered three times a day by smartly uniformed postmen who used the famous postman's knock. The last round was nine o'clock at night, all for a penny stamp on a letter and a halfpenny on a post card. Now that postage has reached an astronomical height, deliveries are far less frequent and the postman's knock has gone.

On the corner facing the station entrance was another grocer's which dealt largely in pennorths and haporths, broken biscuits and the like. You took your basin for a pennorth of treacle, jam or pickles. Next door was a cookshop, meat and two veg for sixpence, pudding a penny extra. Then came a crowded little shop kept by a crusty old man with a peg leg. Here could be had kites, tops, hoops, dolls, mouth organs, jews' harps, celluloid buttons of Boer War favourites, fireworks for the Fifth and Boat Race favours, which we never missed; with ginger beer in the summer and hot cordials a penny a glass in the winter.

A symptom of the times was a collection of louts who used to congregate at the top of the road. Presently one would hear a stampede denoting that a policeman had appeared on the scene. Why they scampered off I do not know, because if they lived aimless lives through lack of work they were certainly not thugs. Every now and then one would disappear to turn up in the uniform of H.M.'s Army, either a line regiment or with the whipstawk—as a whip handle was known in Suffolk—denoting the artillery. It was these poor unfortunates who could be heard on our station platform saying goodbye to their womenfolk as they passed into that "contemptible little army" and a grave in France.

Incidentally, you could see a copper in daylight and smell one

Myself aged about two. A note on the back written by my mother reads, "I think he is a little like Father and me"

Anerley station. St Hugh's Road, where we lived, runs down behind the pub on the left

My mother

at night by reason of his bull's eye lantern burning colza oil and clipped to his belt. Two or more were usually on duty when the pubs closed on a Saturday night and the fights began.

The last time I was able to pay a visit to our street I found the demolition contractors had moved in, and save for a little house here and there where the inhabitants had refused to relinquish their freeholds, St Hugh's and the slightly more respectable Ridsdale Road were in a process of being pulled down. I felt a little sad because I realized that our way of life had completely passed. Those old costermongers' barrows, which had been in use for centuries in old London had become museum pieces, the hoarse cries had ceased, the bell of the rag and bone man was silenced as also that of the muffin man; even the lamplighter's stick was no more. All had gone with the wind to be supplanted by other ways and other manners; in conjunction with village life of centuries, with piped water, electricity and main drainage. Has happiness increased thereby? The question remains unanswered.

> Times go by turns, and chances change by course,
> From foul to fair, from better hap to worse.
>
> ROBERT SOUTHWELL

# 3

# Our Home

The sober comfort, all the peace which springs
From the large aggregate of little things;
On these small cares of daughter, wife or friend,
The almost sacred joys of home depend.

HANNAH MOORE

Number eight St Hugh's Road was a terrace house, near the top of the road, having a short flight of steps running up to the front door. In the lower step which was wider, was a circular hole leading into a damp cellar that was not used. The houses lower down had longer flights of steps until the level was reached. This meant that our lower room, where we lived, was a semi-basement. The room behind, which was really the kitchen was used as my father's workshop. Here in summer Mother did her cooking on an old beatrice stove, otherwise it was done on the fire in our living-room. At some period of its existence Mother had used the iron kitchen range but as the wooden mantel-shelf was draped with cretonne the latter caught alight and nearly set the place on fire. Therefore the range was never used again, so Mother relied on saucepans or a frying-pan. This room looked out on to our garden which was almost in a well.

By the back door was a scullery where there was an old copper not often used, and a sink where we washed in the morning in a wooden tub with sloping sides, as used in the country. Here with the soap was a piece of pumice stone which Father used for his hands, as in spite of doing dirty work he liked clean hands.

Upstairs by the hall door was our sitting-room where visitors were entertained. It was furnished above the average because of certain bequests that came when I was young. There was a spindle-rail couch in American cloth with an arm chair to match, a square table that took up the middle of the room and a small round table in the window, with four mahogany chairs for meals. The window was hung with heavy curtains at the side and lace curtains tied back with a sash. From this window we could watch the life of the road and in season the fine display of fireworks from the Crystal Palace above the tops of the houses opposite. A special occasion vividly remembered was the yacht race for the *America*'s Cup that Sir Thomas Lipton tried so hard to win. We used to herald his green rockets with joy.

This room had folding doors on its inner side, leading into the next room which was our parents' bedroom. When I was very young they had an old mahogany bedstead which had been a half-tester—that is it had once held a canopy partially covering the bed. This ponderous old thing took up nearly the whole of the room, leaving two small recesses by the fireplace. One of these held a chest of drawers of painted oak with white knobs, a doyley on top and a looking glass the side knobs of which would not hold, so that the glass would come forward. Later on Mother persuaded Father to let her buy an iron bedstead with brass knobs and a wire mattress, so the old bed went for firewood.

Above this was my bedroom which looked on to the railway. I had a period piece of an iron tester bed with palliasses and feather bed. At one time it had white dimity curtains, but Mother grew out of these and in my great wisdom later on I cut off the head uprights and spoilt its lines. My dressing-table was a bow-fronted deal table covered with pink glazed chintz and then with a white muslin, with a looking-glass on top. By the side of my bed was my mother's box with which she came to London. This was covered with black American cloth and studded with coffin nails. Here I kept my clothes.

Next door was my brother's room, the blinds of which I still remember because of the design; its outlook was on to the street. Another little room next door was either a box room or a small bedroom. On this top landing was another small staircase which led to yet another little room, probably intended for use by a maid, but for me was a delightful little hideaway with a splendid view on to the railway station. My brother had adorned the walls with all kinds of pictures, making them into a glorified scrap-book. Besides that, as Mother was a hoarder, it was also full of all sorts of bits and pieces: papers, annuals, even old calendars. This was the little room that had a direct hit by one of Hitler's small bombs which blew it to pieces.

Our only light was from oil lamps or from candles. Since the lamps were none too clean or new the resultant light was not too glaring. How we managed I cannot now imagine but as we knew nothing better no hardships were suffered. Father would work with a lamp on his bench in the winter evenings, a tin contraption with a crinkled tin reflector behind the lamp-glass. There was no gas in the house, not even when it finally fell so we had no rimy smell such as was given out by those early gas stoves. But our ceilings were seldom white, bearing the marks of the lamp.

The plumbing was as primitive as the lighting, our water supply coming from a tank set in a lean-to directly over our W.C. And that tank was never cleaned out. In those severe winters when all the pipes were frozen it was necessary to erect standpipes in the road to enable us to get water. Bathing was done once a week, carried out in a galvanized bath. Since this had to rest out of doors it was often the object of cats and the smell was not of bath salts. The soap was Sunlight or Old Brown Windsor. The lavatory was above the sink, a built-in affair of mahogany in a tiny cubicle, and the pan was a study in blue of the flowers of the field. I have just read in Roger Ful-ford's *Hanover to Windsor* that "The Prince's courtiers noticed certain uncomfortable frugalities in the Castle-newspapers in the W.C's". So we were not the only ones to use them. We were a reading family and had a goodly collection of books, some of which must sound a bit queer to modern minds. The family's favourite—not mine—was *Pilgrim's Progress.* We also had Thomson's *The Seasons,* Hervey's *Meditations Among the Tombs,* Queen Victoria's *Leaves from our Life in the Highlands* from my great-uncle's home in Highbury together with a whole host of Methodist imponderables and of course a dour large volume known as a Doctor's Book. Not all of these were read but we followed that excellent practice of reading aloud. We spent our leisure hours hunched round the fire reading, munching sweets if we had any or roasting chestnuts.

We had many callers because Mother kept open house. Her two sisters had become servants in our locality and our home was their home. It was to us they came for their little leisure and alternate Sundays off, when the conversation would be of cooks and their uncertain temperament, and sometimes they would bring their fellow servants or their friends.

One of Mother's visitors was the sister of a naval officer who had been for a spell in service with Mother. She was a precise well-spoken woman, typically Victorian and something of an invalid. Needless to say, her advent called for the best possible show of crockery, plate and napery, and since our home had been enriched by these things from Highbury Mother was able to make some sort of a spread and the splash was made in our upstairs sitting-room and not in the semi-basement.

A Sunday visitor was a certain Sally Beauchamp. She was a wonderful person, never allowing her tongue to remain silent from the moment she set foot in our sitting-room until she departed. She had frizzy golden hair, wore ear-rings that for ever shook, a large gold watch pinned to her high-necked black silk bodice that had a white corded edge round the neck, a brooch containing hair of someone long dead and a row of buttons that ran in a line from waist to throat. She was a great admirer of her mistress and the family, and there would be constant reference to Mrs S—E—P—S and Master S—P who was a budding doctor. It was a doctor's house and the name has been in the news of recent years in connection with the Royal Family.

Another visitor who eventually came to us as a refuge was a short sallow-faced woman with sharp beady eyes. She was a cook and one of my aunts was a parlour maid under her. They lived in a tall house in Belvedere Road and I can remember going there with Mother and sitting spell-bound in that spotless kitchen. It was scrubbed white, the dresser with its load, the table and the chairs. Equally shining were the steel stove with its brass taps, the fender, the graduated covers for the hot meals, the circular knife cleaner, the round-faced clock; not forgetting the Doulton water filter and the beetle trap. Cockroaches were a scourge of kitchens in those days.

I sat there hardly daring to move, asking no questions subconsciously fearful of the greatness that dwelt upstairs. That house passed through three generations of ladies in succession and remained a perfect example of a Victorian home of the upper class until the second war.

The cook and aunt had started with the first lady, she was the Maltese wife of a retired naval doctor. Soon after Aunt's appearance he had died suddenly but his widow carried on. Sometimes Aunt was summoned to go shopping, when the procedure would be—"Rebecca! Put on your best bonnet and we will go to town." They would then proceed to the station, Madam would take a first-class ticket for herself and a third-class for Aunt. When they arrived, they would meet up again, and Aunt would become the parcel-bearer often carrying a great number of packages.

When the widow died the house and contents passed to another Maltese woman, a spinster with a yapping spiteful little dog. Neither cook nor parlour maid could stand Fido snapping at their heels and they had the temerity to complain. Such was the domestic situation, then, that after an interval both got the sack for daring to dislike the pet. What was more, a younger aunt in service nearby was to overhear the lady in question telling the tale of their dismissal to friends when dining out. Whether stating the case for triumph or amusement is not known.

I understand the dog became a bit of a burden especially on wet nights. The lady conceived the bright idea of letting it out on the end of a long piece of string from the top of the steps; but as the animal wandered round the bushes it got rather tangled up. Later she had a large dog which she would take with her on visits away. This had the indecency of dying on her whilst away so she had it boxed up and sent home by carrier. The man's remark as he delivered it was—"I don't know what you've got in here, ma'am, but that's wunnerful heavy and that kind o' smells!"

But I must not omit a good old Christian soul with a shining face, by name Lucy Underwood, who came to us fairly frequently. The memory of her is framed in kindness and good intent. She had a small round head, complete with bun, giving her the appearance of a tranquil Chinese woman.

Sundry old men came to see Father and chatter with him about old times, since every generation has its old times. One was a man who had been employed as a stonemason at the Crystal Palace but was made redundant when it declined. What he lived on I don't know but he and Father always found something to talk about even if it was only that the old days were best.

Then there was an old chemist with the peculiar name of Troake who was a member of our chapel. He would come and sit amid the dust and the hanging lasts and cobbler's trimmings for a little comfort, because he was not always confident about his place in heaven. My Father was no philosopher although his trade was always credited with producing such, yet somehow the old man would go away feeling better.

A doctor, retired from a practice in the Old Kent Road, a pious man with a wife like an ex-Gaiety girl, was Mother's class leader, and came periodically to pray with her. The minister made a duty call when first appointed, after which we saw him no more save at chapel.

But one little demure, black-coated gentleman called each week or once a fortnight peddling tea done up in little white packets. His name was Morrison, some relation to Morrison the missionary. He lived unmarried with his spinster sisters who seemed to dominate him. Mother used to entertain him and he was given the use of our parlour in which to eat his sandwiches. He had an unfortunate catch-phrase, pointed out to me by my brother with evil intent. It was, "Indeed truly, that's very certain". Of course I disgraced myself if it came out when I was one of the listeners. Poor gentle creature, it was said also by my brother that once long years ago Mr Morrison had designs on our mother, but his sisters would not allow what they considered a marriage beneath him. Not having the courage of his affections he lost the prize and went lonely to his grave. How my brother knew I don't know.

Father's workshop was the old kitchen that looked out on to our back yard. There he sat on a stool that once had been a Windsor chair with a back, from eight o'clock in the morning until six o'clock at night, or even later. He wore the traditional leather apron and his lapstone was the base of a sad iron. His bench, a home-made contraption fashioned from an egg box was in front of the window littered with grimy tools amid which his very sharp knives glinted with almost sinister aspect. The window ledge served as the upper platform of the bench on the edge of which was his little oil lamp, always alight, so contrived as to hold his finishing irons. To the astringency of leather was added the aromatic smell of melted wax or heelball. By his side was a pail of water, dark and silent like a mountain pool. In this he softened his leather; and on the bare walls flanking the window hung his wooden lasts, thick with dust. They had been inherited from his previous employer, together with a couple of signs in oval frames which spoke of "Bespoke Orders" and

"Spring-Sided Boots a Speciality". They would be valuable museum pieces today.

Father had no machinery and all his sewing was done by hand, with the aid of bristles and sharply curved awls like the beak of an avocet. He would even make his own waxed thread and I have so often watched him doing this with a lump of beeswax and hempen twine. Sewing was hard work, inserting the bristles one against the other in the hole made in a channel of the sole by another tool and then pulling the stitch tight. For this work he wore a leather mitten covering the centre of his hand, and as his threads were released from the pull so there would be a tearing sound and he would bare his teeth.

The finishing process of boots and shoes, newly soled and heeled, fascinated me. The skin of the new leather was buffed off with a broken portion of a steel blade, then the sole was rubbed with sandpaper, bleached with oxalic acid rubbed on with a cork bung, and carefully heelballed along the edges and the instep with one or two of his hot irons. Finished, it was a job well done and made a man proud of his work. The boots were then tied up in neat parcels and it was my job a little later in life to take them home in a brown canvas sack slung over my shoulders. When negotiating the dark recesses of some of our ill-lit roads, I would bolster up my courage with a whistle.

Father sat and worked amid a deposit of leather cuttings, old worn soles and the impedimenta of his trade. This debris came in handy for our fire, and I remember it burnt with a lovely opalescent flame. He was at his best when he received a bespoke order for a pair of new boots. After all, that was what he was trained for. He would then spruce himself up, take his slide rule and a notebook and present himself at his client's front door. He would handle the feet with the greatest care and under-standing noting all the tender spots and deformities such as bunions, enlarged joints and corns. Returning home he would take down a pair of his lasts, approximating to size and proceed to transfer to them the peculiarities of the feet he had been examining. This was done by bits of leather fastened on by tingles (small sharp tacks) and shaved to shape. When completed he would have a fair copy of his client's feet on which to build.

These orders necessitated a trip to town to buy the uppers which were of box calf or kid, and sundry bits of grindery needed in the boots' fashioning. When he settled down to the job it would take him the best part of a week, hard at it, almost all sewing, the only nails being in the heels. There was one essential thing about a boot, it must not let in water, in fact the whole genius seemed to lie in the welt, the narrow piece of leather between the sole and the upper. By a curious twist of speech, when well made the boots would fit like a glove. Of course there were plenty of folk in those days who declared they couldn't wear a ready-made boot.

And this raises the question, where have all the squeaky boots gone to? They were quite numerous and could be heard in melody along our streets, particularly so in a public building such as a church, if the wearer happened to be a sidesman. Folks said it denoted that the boots (shoes were not much in vogue then) had not been paid for.

There was an art in cutting out the soles and heels from a butt of leather. This was done from little paper templates filed off from the boot in work, to prevent waste.

# 4

# Our Old London and Brighton Railway

As a poor boy and with no choice in the matter, I was born in a really remarkable spot, because our house backed on to a railway station and my bedroom window looked on to the platforms, while our front looked towards the Crystal Palace and the fireworks that could be seen above the tree tops opposite. What more could anyone want? As a family we were never lonely, because that railway was a great companion and the smartest, proudest little line in the country. It was our friend, our weather guide (as to which way the wind blew the smoke), clock, and outlook into the world in general. It was busy for eighteen hours out of the twenty-four, if not longer; and the friendly nature of those old trains as they trundled to London Bridge northwards and as far afield as Brighton southwards (then a terribly long way off), was beyond reckoning. They linked us with Queen Victoria, Lord Mayors, Old Father Thames, the green fields, rolling Downs and the white cliffs of England. (And the London Coal Exchange). We knew the railway language, spoke its jargon and entered into its life. In fact we were so closely connected with it that our little back yard was fenced off at its extremity by old tarred railway sleepers, standing upright, close together and capped with triangular-shaped planks. As the bolt-holes were still in the sleepers, we could thrust in an iron rod and so climb to the top to view the forbidden land.

Between our garden and the platforms, which were on a

much higher level, was a green bank, so delightfully green for such a grubby street as ours. There grew all kinds of grasses and wild flowers reaching perfection in the crown of the year. Totty grass (also called quaking grass), moon daisies, snap-dragons, bird's-eye, campion, blue meadow-sweet, crane's-bill, and all the others. Then, without warning, the reapers would appear and mow down the lot, turning it into hay for the rail-way horses. And we were that much the poorer. Even then, however, it was good to look at and to smell. A splendid rowan tree flourished and overhung the station platform, directly over the name-board, and a row of luxurious limes grew at the bottom of the bank, just beyond the fence. It is true they tended to darken the lower rooms of the houses, but they were verdant in spring.

Our outlook was just clear of these limes, but over the fence was a bed of blackberries, the envy of all the neighbours and the especial pride of the station-master's wife. Someone with a basin might creep along and gather the lot when she was not looking, or before the porters had noticed.

But there was something else, an immense span of telegraph wires ran beside that line, becoming in turn a vast Aeolian harp to be played by every wind that blew; or at times to be dotted by notes that were in reality perching birds, or men spread-eagled like flying monsters.

Those railway embankments held a rare fascination for boys, probably because of their great length and because they pre-sented dangers—they were forbidden areas, with notice boards bearing the signature of the general manager threatening dire penalties if caught.

When I was very young an approaching train was heralded by a bell rung from the signal box at the southern end of the up-platform. The train arrived, the porters would walk up and down the platform singing out the list of stations at which the train would stop—Penge, Sydenham, Forest Hill, Honor Oak Park, Brockley, New Cross, London Bridge. Then the doors would be slammed to and the handles turned, for there were no automatic locks, and another porter would give three or four vigorous turns to a handbell that stood rim downwards on the platform. It was a serious business receiving and flagging away a passenger train in those days. The last train from the station was very late at night, after which all the lights were turned out one at a time. The first train was correspondingly early in the morning. On Sundays, however, the railway was quieter, because stopping trains were restricted, as they were not allowed to run during the hours of divine service. Consequently the last train up from our station for a considerable interval was about ten-thirty in the morning.

It was the engines on our line that were our pride and joy, painted light brown and lined and streaked with brass; and on the sides the name of a station on the system. We were not very old before we had got that alphabet: A for Amberley, B for Balcombe, C for Chichester, and so on, all linked with a serial number. I wish today I had the old black shiny covered folding notebook with its elastic band, into which I copied those I spotted from our topmost attic window, as they drew up at the station or flew past in a plume of smoke. But those engines held something else, of which I was unaware at the time. In the cabin was the name of the driver and the mileage he had driven. All this pride stemmed from a manager named Stroudly, who treated his engines as a work of art.

Another great attraction of that railway was the signalling. Great baulks of timber reared aloft, carrying a staging almost like a ship's mast. Plain or forked semaphores were used and the twinkling lights. So often have I watched the porter making his way along the platform with a paper flambeau, knocking it into life when he had climbed up the ladder and reached the lamps; no automatic lighting then. Moreover, we were so close to that railway that when we heard the signal drop for a local train, we had time to run round and catch it. Needless to say we did nothing of the sort, for catching a train was an event and one allowed an ample margin for the play of the imagination and suspense.

Anerley Bridge was the best vantage spot from which to view that railway. I can just remember the old bridge with corrugated-iron walls that had been sufficiently wide to take the ambling traffic of those early years. It was altered, strengthened and widened to take the trams when they came in all their flashing splendour. From this bridge the line could be seen in both directions, as far as Penge northwards, and Norwood Junction southwards. A lot of light went to the making of Norwood, and that junction seemed the centre of fairyland. How strange that time has ruthlessly swept away those twinkling lights and that form of signalling.

I didn't know then that the Brighton railway was famed for its signalling, that the first adaptation of the semaphore to railway signalling was made by Charles Hutton Gregory at New Cross in 1842. That the notched end of the distant arm, known as a fishtail, was first proposed by Superintendant W. J. Williams and used at Norwood Junction. I was unaware, until I read Mr Ellis's book that our signal posts were so graceful in their white and red paint and their clerical-looking hats. You see, we took it all for granted as being part of our civilization and our way of life. Enough for us that the arms rose and fell, and the whistling, steaming, little brown engines rushed past, or chugged with heavy and mysteriously shaped loads through the night. It was enough too, that the line was all clear for the 'Brighton Fast', as also for the Race Special that bore a placard on the front of the engine.

Our bit of line from London Bridge to Croydon was the oldest stretch of the London Railway. It was commenced in 1836 and opened on 5th June 1839. The Company purchased the Croydon Canal for £42,000, the bed of which was used as the track. The engineer was Joseph Gibbs, and the total outlay £528,000. There was a level-crossing at Penge, where a policeman was stationed to attend to the gates, and there was another at 'The Jolly Sailor', South Norwood.

In 1846, the railway was the subject of an experiment to run on air. This was carried out by the brothers Joseph and Jacob Samuda, and a man named Clegg. Before it was finished, Jacob died and Clegg went to Portugal, leaving Joseph to finish the job.

Pumping stations were erected at intervals, in which were large air pumps driven by steam engines. There was one of these at Forest Hill, and another at the Goat House, Norwood Junction. This accounted for the rather magnificent appearance of Forest Hill station until the Second World War almost laid it waste. The trains were of the ordinary variety of those days, but the leading vehicle was fitted with an arm that slotted into the pipe. William Cubitt recommended the adoption of this system to the London and Croydon Railway.

There had been a difficulty in finding names for the stations, so two were named after local inns, 'The Dartmouth Arms', Forest Hill, and 'The Jolly Sailor' at Norwood Junction. Anerley, meaning 'lonely', because of its isolation, was so called by a Scottish merchant who had built a house there on a small estate.

Because of the nature of the country through which the line passed, the stations and buildings received special treatment. It was said they were amongst the most beautifully designed of their kind. They were the work of an architect, W. H. Breakspear, who chose the Early English period for examples. The station houses resembled churches and the chimneys of the pumping stations looked like campaniles or slender bell-towers, presumably under the influence of the Gothic Revival then greatly in evidence. Those at Forest Hill, Norwood and Croydon, were erected by Peto and Grissel, the local contractors. When the line was extended to Epsom, the style of half-timbered houses was adopted. This influence can still be seen in the little cottage on the up-side at Anerley, wherein lived the station-master of our day. It is worth a glance as the pages are turned.

It was evidently a very interesting bit of engineering, because an air cylinder from this Croydon Atmospheric Railway is preserved at the York Railway Museum.

Anerley Gardens, opened in 1841, were on the site of Ridsdale and St Hugh's Roads. These were evidently a small edition of the Ranelagh and Vauxhall Gardens, but were closed through abuse.

That brings us to London Bridge Station, the first railway terminus in London, built in the Regency style in 1836 by G. Smith, a little-known architect. It was extended to serve the traffic that would result when the Crystal Palace was moved from Hyde Park to Sydenham. Some of the earlier portion remains to this day in spite of being hammered by enemy bombs. The Crystal Palace branch was opened on the 10th June 1854, running over our famous Penge Tunnel and crossing Beckenham Road by a very fine viaduct.

How far away and long ago it all seems, since as a little boy, I scrambled up very early in the morning by candlelight, and went to this London Bridge station with my lame father. London was a magic place to me; in fact the way up also added joy to joy as we stopped at the stations, the names of which I had memorized by constant callings out. And then, after New Cross, with my imagined memories of Dickens who worked in Day and Martin's blacking factory in view across the platforms, we skimmed the roof tops and the forest of twisted chimney pots, passing Bermondsey and its smell of leather and such interesting places as a Virgin Vinegar brewery (why "Virgin" I have never been able to understand), and drew into the terminus itself. Our business was done by the afternoon, so having passed the statue of King William IV looking straight across the river to the south bank, we followed his gaze and made our way home again, with joy in reverse. If it was winter and one of those early dark afternoons there was that great sight of being able to watch the porters dropping the pot lamps through the roof of the carriages into a perforated iron cage. Those lamps, burning

My father

The Wesleyan church in Anerley which our family attended

Anerley Road leading to Crystal Palace

rape-oil, looked from the outside like a series of top hats running along the roof of the train. I can also recall the flat, heavylooking feet-warmers that were filled with hot water and must have made travelling in unheated trains in winter slightly more tolerable.

This brings to mind our one great local accident, which happened on May Day, 1891, when I was two. One of the twentyfoot cast-iron spans of the railway bridge crossing Portland Road, South Norwood, gave way. The 8.45 a.m. fast business train was derailed in making the crossing, but the driver managed to pull up. However, it was not before the rear coach fell through and stood on its end in the roadway. Only five people were slightly injured. Needless to say, it was a nine day's wonder. This led to the replacement of all cast-iron spans for bridges.

Holiday time made our station very busy, and as all luggage had to accompany the passenger, and most passengers seemed to need a great many things, and as holidays were taken *en famille*, the resultant encumbrance was enormous. The stuff would be piled high and wheeled about on those immense sack barrows, the trunks bearing all kinds of strange names, such as saratogas and imperials. Then there were cabin trunks and always those domed top baskets covered with black shiny leather cloth, hat boxes for both sexes, carpet bags; and, of course, Gladstone bags as hand luggage. Neither should we forget the pathetic-looking tin trunk of the servant maid, always japanned to simulate oak, like the old chests of drawers. There would even be baths, hip and sponge, with wicker linings, and lids fastened on with straps. These served two purposes, a personal bath for our old retired army officers, and something in which to transport their personal necessaries.

And last of all, the platforms were lined with primitive forms of advertisements, for the bald announcements to be found in the columns of the daily papers had counterparts on enamelled sheets of tin. There was a splash of blue-black across one, inscribed "Stephen's Inks", a railway guard's lantern on another with a well-defined beam that flashed on to "Hudson's Soap". Not forgetting another labelled "Monkey Brand Soap", with a shining frying-pan and a reminder that it wouldn't wash clothes. There was also one bit of lyricism that announced—"The Pickwick, the Owl and the Waverley Pen, come as a boon and a blessing to men", the use of which, be it remembered, was the goal of our schooldays.

# 5

# Our Suburbia

There was an old person of Anerley,
Whose conduct was strange and unmannerly;
   He rushed down the Strand
   With a pig in each hand,
But returned in the evening to Anerley.

EDWARD LEAR

Our locality must have been a very pleasant place when our Father and Mother set up house there. Like so many other suburbs on the fringe of London it was semi-rural in character, and in their young days could only have been newly built; one supposes it rose and fell with the Crystal Palace. There were brickfields near at hand, in Versailles Road, while near our cemetery at Elmers End, Featherley's Stock Bricks were being produced.

Leafing the pages of an old directory I find there were sundry harness-makers, a collar-dresser (horse), a carriage-builder, brickmaker, laundryman, window-blind maker, a turnery and brush-maker, wireworker and an ivory-turner; a wheelwright on one side of Hartfield Grove and a farrier on the other.

Then there were corset-makers, a dress- and mantle-maker, umbrella-maker and hatter. A Mrs Brimmer made dairy utensils. After all, there were buttermen in those days as well as cheese-mongers. Perchance Mrs Brimmer catered for the numerous dairies, all of which had rural designations, such as Oak Farm, Berkshire Farm, Maple Farm, Hayes Farm and College Farm.

There was a brewery functioning in my time, filling the air with the fragrance of malt and barley once or twice a week.

One sweep lived down our street but the others had developed into Chimney Cleaners. I can just remember their activities as Jack-in-the-Green, taking a stance before our old inns of 'The Crooked Billet', 'Hop Pole', 'Royal Oak' and 'The Dew Drop'. There were furniture dealers and furniture brokers and a toll-gate keeper in Kent House Lane. Also a goodly number of fancy goods repositories presumably kept by bespectacled spinsters, always in a muddle, but full of that Victoriana that is so much sought after today.

I can also remember certain little shops of an intriguing character, such as dairies with milking sheds behind and butchers' shops with pent-house windows and slaughterhouses at the side.

Now that all roads are covered with tarmac and the majority of people have never known anything else, it is difficult to recall their condition when I was young. They were macadamized it is true, but their surface was of grit and the resultant clouds of dust in summer, the pot holes and the extraordinary size of the puddles in winter appear incredible as one looks back. In those hot summers, notably the now legendary dog days, the water cart was a welcome feature, sprinkling the roads and laying the dust for a minute or two. Moreover, since the traffic was horse-drawn they were littered with horse droppings, which when swept into heaps and mixed with dust became the famous London manure.

Then as now our streets received the attention of sundry labourers who tore up the surface of the roads creating holes for the passer-by to gaze into. But there was something music-ally fine about their endeavours. These gangs were an interesting lot and their muscularity astounding. They wore bell-bottomed trousers with pipe-stem legs, raised seams and fall fronts. A chisel would be held by one of them by means of a twisted withy and the remainder would form a ring with their sledge-hammers each striking in turn. The result was a series of ring-ing blows that in effect rivalled the efforts of the company of ringers in the belfry. They usually smoked a short clay pipe, or nose warmer as it was called, and carried their food in an old matting frail basket. At meal time they would gather round the brazier fire, cook a two-eyed steak, or a rasher of bacon and eat it laid on a huge slice of bread, their pocket knives providing a thumb bit at a mouthful.

An extremely interesting feature was the tipcart, without which the cartage of sand, gravel and rubble could not have been accomplished. These one-horsed carts held a yard of sand when evenly and fully loaded and one horse could manage it quite well. The stuff had to be thrown in by hand shovels but the unloading was easy. There was a pin at the rear of the shafts, the tailboard was removed, the pin taken out and the contents shot on the ground. The horse knew, moved one pace forward and the cart emptied. These old carters always worked in line ahead, the leading horse knew the way if the others didn't. With the passing of the horse there passed away that wonderful race of drivers and the world will never see their like again.

There was a good deal of noise, since the iron-shod wheels ground over the raw surface and the horses clip-clodded in unison. Later there was a movement towards muffling the noise and making private carriages a little more smooth in transit by the addition of solid rubber tyres, but this did not apply to vans and heavy vehicles. Curiously enough roads were dangerous even then and folks got run over. Neither must we forget that peculiar little pose, for it could have been nothing more, strewing straw in the road outside a house where someone lay sick, as also the muffling of the door knocker. Gloom and tragedy seemed to be mingled with the straw.

The miry state of the roads gave rise to a peculiar race, not large in numbers but gentle in mien, the crossing sweeper. I feel perfectly sure on looking back that many of them must have been old soldiers. Often they were minus a leg or an arm, and might have at times a child or an old dog to assist their plaintive habit of extracting coppers into the cap lying near their box seat. (Also there were men with a hook instead of a hand, always known as "Hookey so-and-so").

A really terrifying moment in those old streets was occasioned by runaway horses. I can hear the awful drumming of hooves even now. This called forth very great heroism which was never lacking in those often despised policemen. Another, and really exciting episode was the fire engine. This upright brass engine, the fire in its belly being lit by a brass-hatted fireman at the rear, was drawn by bus horses and I believe the firemen were roadmen. There were also boneshaker bicycles to be seen with rude boys shouting "Old iron never rusts, Solid tyres never bust". But the early motorcars began to appear, and it might be recalled that the famous "Guards to Hastings" run was organized by the Automobile Association in 1909, which had only been in existence for four years.

Anerley is part of Penge but has no parochial boundaries and yet has a station. Indeed, it is said to owe its existence to that station and to the enterprise of a former proprietor of the manor, a Mr Anerley. Its entity was really cultural, providing a lodgement for the wealthier and more intellectual. I had to go over the bridge to do the shopping for Mother, to Sunday School and twice daily to school. There was a constant stream over the bridge, since all of our part of the world passed at some time or another even if it was on that last journey, for the way led to the cemetery.

I was intrigued to read that when courting, Mr and Mrs Beeton used to meet on the bridge before making their way to the Crystal Palace. Isabella Mayson would come up from Epsom where she lived in the Grand Stand, while Samuel Beeton would arrive from London. And poor Isabella was dead before she was twenty-nine. She lies in that crowded West Norwood cemetery, not far from Blondin and his rope.

Just by the bridge stands the Town Hall. It boasts an illumin-ated clock which has been most useful and has stood two world wars. Here met our vestry whose one function was to keep down the rates. This later expanded into an Urban District Council and the rates expanded likewise. The ground at the rear and the buildings adjoining were those of the North Surrey District Schools ruled over by a Board of Guardians. Here the boys were taught farming in the fields of several acres, boot-making, baking, tailoring; while the girls were trained as servants. It was also a jumping-off ground for the colonies and the army, since they had quite a nice little band that sometimes played at local functions.

Justice was not meted out at the Town Hall but at a curious little low building at the top of Jasmine Grove adjoining the Royal Oak. It had been a billiards room, but was turned into a Court House. The time to watch that unpretentious little place was the Monday morning after the Cup Final at the Crystal Palace. A whole line of pick-pockets, card-sharpers and trick-sters of all kinds took up the time of the magistrates for some hours.

The shops along the Anerley Road, from the bridge turning to the right were, first of note, a baker's, the proprietor of which described himself as a "Pastry Cook and Rout Furnisher". I puzzled over the latter for a long time until I entered my appren-ticeship when I discovered we lent out rout-seats, which were long stools with cane tops to seat four or six persons, and that a rout was a ball. If one attended this shop early enough one could line up (as I had to do) with a raggle-taggle band and get two-pennyworth of stale bread. What the girls shovelled into one's bag was a glorious lucky dip of rolls, milk loaves and enough bread to last for days. Then came a chemist's where I was an errand boy for a time, waiting in the cellar for calls. A greengrocer's came next, the owner was a member of our church. Mother said he had a girl's behind. A pennyworth of specked apples or oranges was by no means to be despised.

A piano shop provided musical instruments, a very nice boot and shoe shop sold the best makes, an ironmonger's was stocked from floor to ceiling and then came a fishmonger's staffed by a family who wore the traditional straw hats. The time to see this at its very best was at Christmas, when the whole front was aglow with turkeys, ducks and geese, many bearing rosettes won at a show. It was a wonderful sight even if it was dimmed by a pea-soup fog. The ground was plentifully strewn with saw-dust.

Now came two of especial note, one was a grocer's and the other a draper's, both of which must have been built when I was a babe. It was a delight to enter the grocer's and I like to recall its gleaming mahogany, its shining tin canisters and the urbanity of all within; it was also a post office where my first and only account was opened. After eighty odd years that has only just been changed in form.

The shop, magnificent as it was, had a sawdust floor and was divided into the usual departments, a new one I can remember being for brooms and brushes. It is hardly necessary to say the goods were weighed and packed as required, that bacon was slithered off by hand with a rapier-like knife and cheese cut with amazing accuracy of weight. The bacon went on to scales with a marble platform that wobbled and was weighed by pillar weights of shining brass; while the tea was put into little brass scoops and weighed with flat round weights. They are all museum-pieces today. The bacon man wore a white apron with a torn fringe across the waist, while I think the grocery men wore a plain white apron. And, of course, there was the pleasant smell of spice, with coffee predominating. That shop had a smart set of ponies and little boxes on wheels which ran about our best roads. They were stabled at the top of our road in what had been an old sorting office. The establishment was founded by a Mr Walker Smith who died before my time and was succeeded by his son who was killed serving with the London Scottish.

Next door was the draper's, equal in many ways to the grocer's, presided over by a magnificent person named Grose and an equally mysterious one named Smith. It was a bright shop claiming some quality; and the lady customers sat on tall cane-seated chairs and put their dainty feet on a brass-bound ledge that ran along the base of the counters. The shop front had more brass in the form of ornate storeboards, all of which had to be kept clean and shiny. They had a man to do this, one of those curious undefined beings that such establishments seemed to create. When not so employed he would take out the orders in a band-box slung across his shoulders by a leather strap, and then at the close of day put up the shutters and generally secure everything against burglars that never did and never would raid such a place.

There was a tale running concerning the draper. He was re-puted to have courted his wife, a pleasant little woman, clandes-tinely at the local railway station. She was the ward of an old pinched couple who had made a fortune out of umbrellas, and hangers-on were not encouraged. However they were married, they did inherit the fortune and they did live happily ever after-wards.

Turning back on one's tracks and crossing the bridge, one came first to a bank, then an off-licence which is still there, another boot and shoe shop run by a woman, a chemist who had the biggest bald head for miles around, but was a very nice man, a florist's and last a butcher's, whose owner was called Glass. I had to go there for six-pennyworth of pieces (known as 'block ornaments'), or chump chops. His shop also had a saw-dust floor.

Down the other side of the railway was a grocer's where I was sent for butter which was patted up as required. The name was Milton and they were a very nice family who belonged to our church, two sons and two daughters. A tobacco shop came next where cigarettes were sold by the ounce, loose. Here was another of our church families kept going by a very brave woman with a sick husband. He had been a schoolmaster but had some incurable disease. He lay on a couch in the shop. When he died his wife took in young men from Methodist families who had come to London in white collar jobs. There were two sons and a daughter. I was friendly with the younger of the boys who was to become one of the general managers of Barclays Bank; all three did well.

Next door was an undertaker's, a very prosperous business which had developed from a carpenter's shop at Upper Norwood. Here was another nice family, the two boys attending my school. Alas, alas, I fear the whisky bottle did for them both. Moving down the shops was a hairdresser's with a woman's bust in the window and an announcement that ladies' trimmings were made up. I used to go there for a haircut, although they charged a shilling because they used a mechanical brush that felt so nice. I fear it was exhausting to the poor man who had to use it. It was worked from a hand engine in the corner which set in motion a rail on the ceiling from which hung endless rings of rubber into which the brush was inserted.

Passing down the hill came a sweet shop, a watch and clock maker's, an oil and colour shop where I first became acquainted with incandescent light and where we bought our paraffin oil. This was kept by a little gingery man who manipulated the funds of the Penge Perseverance Building Society. Next came a corn chandler's and a baker's of long standing.

Crossing the road was a pawnbroker's exhibiting the three brass balls and patronized on a Monday morning by women; also a paper shop. Here too was an old-time draper, a perfectly urbane person who, I think, wore a frock-coat and was helped by his daughters, one of which was a somewhat affected lady. By the station entrance was a cab rank, and cabmen's shelter. There was nothing more depressing on a wet day than a cab-rank, the horses standing on the stone setts, champing at their nosebags. Opposite was a harness-maker's shop, with the men working in the windows.

Boys at that time were much in evidence, especially the errand boys. They followed their respective trades and carried the goods in specially designed baskets, such as that for wine bottles with separate compartments, or medicine with a lidded basket, grocery in a square basket; the baker's basket was a huge affair and one could tell the weight it held by the creak of the handle. The butcher's boy carried his load on his shoulder on a wooden scooped-out tray that was scrubbed white. These are now classed as antiques and fetch a high price; the fishmonger's boy had a flat tray. These various young rascals might have Saturday jobs or they might be whole timers. In any case they were a merry lot without a care in the world, would sometimes meet with other boys, have a chat or a surreptitious smoke, since time was of no account, and would whistle the latest music-hall refrains.

One job was rather enviable and that was a van-boy's. He travelled at the back of a van and had a rope suspended from the roof by which he could hold on, or assist himself in reaching his place. Sometimes, if so inclined, he would perform a few acrobatics, holding on almost at right angles. (Incidentally the drivers were nearly all ruptured through lifting too heavy weights). Other boys would meet the trains and the outcoming passengers, with "Carry yer bag, sir?" They would walk a mile or two with a heavy package for twopence or threepence. A paper-round brought in a shilling or two, but that had to be handed in.

Boys usually had a Saturday job, often in private houses. These consisted of cleaning knives, forks and spoons, chopping wood and fetching coals. Some of those old shrewish spinsters saw to it they got their money's worth. One such paid threepence a week and gave a never-varying meal of two sausages and two potatoes. For this he had to chop wood in the cellar enough to last a week, clean the knives, forks and spoons, wash and hearth-stone the steps, wash the tessellated forecourt and finally scrub the kitchen and scullery floors which were of bare boards. Another job at a draper's found him confronted with eighteen pairs of boots in the basement. He did these two nights running but his resolution failed on the third. It should be remembered that boots had to be cleaned the hard way with Day and Martin's '97 Blacking', sold in either flat, shiny, round tins or in messy paper skins. The best results were obtained by moistening the black mass with beer dregs, or vinegar, although a little spit was not without virtue. Those old steel knives also had nothing labour saving about them. They were cleaned on a knife board covered with linoleum, that was sprinkled with Oakey's dark and evil-looking powder. If they were not wiped clean after the operation, not forgetting the blade up to the handle, the butter told the tale, since a chocolate cream effect was not appreciated.

Penge had an open-air market in the Maple Road, where you could meet the man from Nottingham hoarsely selling his wares by a series of decreasing price offers. The same tactics were followed by the pottery and china merchant unearthing ceramic treasures from his huge straw-filled crates. His wrath knew no bounds as he descended to the final crash and dashed the pot to pieces since there were no bidders. He was probably unaware of the inscription on an old plate—

> This dish is made of earth,
> When it breaks the potter laughs,
> Therefore take care of it.

Sometimes a circus would come to an open field nearby and part of the attraction was another auction of gimcracks. A nice, pretty little tea-set for instance which might be had for a shilling or two, and as an inducement, since he was a generous salesman, the cheap-jack would slip a golden sovereign into one of the cups. When the purchasers got home and unpacked the treasure they would discover all was not gold that glittered; but it was all part of the fun of the fair.

To this same open space would come that most famous of all quacks—the noted Sequah. He appears in the Darwin *Letters* and this is what a member of the family said of him: "Cambridge is all upside down about Sequah, a quack doctor who holds meetings twice each day and is attended by thousands. The general routine is that a rheumatic man is helped up into the van where he takes a sort of a dram and is rubbed for twenty minutes or so, the band playing loud to drown his cries. He comes out and Sequah asks him to dance which he does. Sequah makes great sums by the sale of his medicines, which is in fact whisky and laudanum or some anodyne. But he also throws about sovereigns and gives them to successful cures; and in one case to an old woman who was not cured, he said, "I can do nothing for you!" It proved to be a five pound note. 'Sequah' is a company with many agents. Young women are anxious to touch him as they believe it will make their love affairs succeed."

There was another and more picturesque feature of the Maple Road. About midway Carter Paterson had their stables. The time to watch the parade of Suffolk Punches, Percherons, etc., was on a May morning when they came out decked in all the arts of the horse milliner. A pretty sight indeed to celebrate so gay an occasion, but you had to be there early.

Penge was known at the 'Holy City', at least that was the epithet given to it by facetious porters at one of the London termini, "Anymore for the 'Holy City'?" would be the cry. It was so called from the many churches and meeting houses within its borders. Some of the Anglican low churches had been endowed by two very wealthy spinster sisters, the Misses Dudin Brown.

The old religion was housed in a somewhat grim-looking building in Padua Road, where it also had a school. The boys, some of Italian origin, sons of marble sculptors for our cemetery, were always more or less at feud with my school. They would waylay and attack us on our homeward ways, although I don't think any harm was done or blood spilt.

In one of our groves lived a man who sold potatoes and wrote verse. I have a small green volume devoted to his muse:

> In Ivy Cottage, Hawthorn Grove,
> Your humble servant dwell.

> I traffic not in gold and gem
> But to the public sell—
> Potatoes, which stand next to bread
> The staff of life to man.
> So if the chance presents itself
> Buy of me if you can.

His name was Joseph Gwyer, first he went bankrupt, then mad and ended his career by throwing himself on the fire.

Just outside our hamlet was an experiment in building material. It was a church constructed of burnt earth derived from local slag heaps, a variety of terracotta concrete. This was dedicated to the doctrines, or visions, of Emanuel Swedenborg, and still exists; I believe it is now a listed building, and serves a very wide area.

A nearby neighbour, living in a typical Victorian detached villa, was Dr Conan Doyle. This penurious Southsea doctor had got over the worst when he pulled up at Tennison Road, South Norwood, and was enabled to live in comfort for the rest of his life on the proceeds of his remarkable creation. So we were really part and parcel of the England that still lives in the Holmes stories. Then in later years in our very midst dwelt that elfish poet Walter de la Mare, as also another of the Georgian poets, John Freeman.

Bank Holidays (instituted by Sir John Lubbock who lived at High Elms, Farnborough, not far from Mr Darwin at Downe), were usually celebrated by a walk to Shirley Hills with Father, who although lame would swing along on his one and only crutch in great style. It was a long drag for small feet, particularly the last mile or so homewards, but it was better than staying at home, and after all we had to go through farmland to get there. We also had to pass through Lloyd's Woods (of weekly-paper fame) before we emerged by Shirley Church with its broach spire. In the churchyard is the marble tomb designed and inscribed by Ruskin for first his father whom he described as "an entirely honest merchant", then his mother: "Here beside my father's body, I have laid my mother's; nor was dearer earth ever returned to earth, nor purer life ever recorded in Heaven". Then came—*Age quod Agis.* (Incidentally, I was the last to take a photograph of their home on Denmark Hill, which duly appeared in *Country Life.*)

Nearby lived the old rector who had produced and cultivated the Shirley poppy. He would be rather shocked if he could return to his sylvan retreat, see the mass of houses and the pub set in the midst named after his delicate and lovely bloom.

On those Shirley Hills lived the last of the Broom Squires that produced the birch brooms, or besoms, sold by our corn chandlers and nurserymen. Just over the hill lay Addington Palace, a one-time country seat of the Archbishops of Canterbury. In the tiny churchyard of the parish church several of them are buried.

Or the walk might be to Hayes Common, where they still crown a Queen of the May, and where stood Hayes Place, once a home of the Pitt family, but now demolished. Holwood Park, seat of the Derby family, was not far away. Amid the trees was the Wilberforce Oak under which the slave question was discussed. Nearby was Keston with its ponds and windmill.

Sometimes the jaunt was to Horniman's Museum at Forest Hill. That was nearer home, it is true, but a jolly long way all the same; and it was the old museum that had been his private house and not the present ugly structure. My childhood memories of that are of an eeriness that seemed to pervade the whole place. It was a bit much to be greeted by some mummified princess on the landing, or by some Hindu god with six arms, one hand holding a raw scalp. But it was a place of never-failing interest.

Anerley Road began (or ended) at four crossways known as the Robin Hood, from an old hostelry of that name that had been the haunt of a lawless crew. It was a spot that had not been safe to pass when darkness came. Before that for many generations it had been a farmhouse which had stood there in a clearing of the wood, recessed from the road. The splendid neo-gothic Church of the Holy Trinity with an immense spire on the opposite corner that had sprung out of the fields of Oak Farm, which only disappeared in 1868, had not yet grown old enough to provide a waymark. During Hitler's blitz a bomb was dropped plumb in the middle of the four ways, which knocked out the church but not the pub.

Travelling up towards the bridge one passed some iron railings and as one peered through, there lying in a verdant setting was a straight piece of water with a rockery fountain in the middle. That was the last remnant of the old canal, that before the railway had linked London and Croydon. On this old piece of water in winter, those severe winters of the eighties and nineties, the young life of Anerley Road and adjacent houses disported itself on skates amid a fairyland of Chinese lanterns. Sometimes in the equally hot summers it was not so enchanting as it was apt to smell.

In many respects Anerley Road was a beautiful thoroughfare. It was known as the Anerley Switchback because it consisted of three separate inclines. When one considers that in those days there were only horses for transport, it was a hard lot for the animals, especially the Anerley Hill portion. How the poor old things struggled and strained as they mounted zigzag, possibly driven by rather callous drivers. Later on as the RSPCA got more powerful, an old army doctor, named Surgeon Major Poole organized a trace-horse that was kept at the top of the hill to help with the loads. This was superseded by a small traction engine which was known as the Little Giant. It was distinctly amusing to watch the reaction of the old horses. First they were rather scared but very soon they accepted the benefit, sat back in their britchens and let the engine pull them up as well.

Nearly at the top of the hill where stood the South Tower was Cintra Park. Here lived old Martin Farquhar Tupper, author of *Proverbial Philisophy*. He had been present at the Mansion House dinner when the projected scheme for the Great Ex-

Penge Triangle, showing the 'Crooked Billet', Watermen's and
Lightermen's Almshouses and St John's Church

High Street, Bagshot

The farm, Bagshot, where my aunt and family lived

Tot and Liz who lived at Green Farm, Bagshot. One had a very high-pitched voice, the other a very low-pitched voice

hibition was inaugurated by the Prince Consort. The Prince told the company that they were living in an age of the most wonderful transition, tending rapidly to the unity of mankind and that the Exhibition would give a living picture of the point of development at which the whole of mankind had arrived, and would be a new starting point for their exertions in the future. Yet Tupper could write:

> Glacier diamond, Alp of glass,
> Sinbad's cave, Alladin's Hall,
> Must it then be crush'd, alas!
> Must the Crystal Palace fall?

That it did fall, all the world knows, in a conflagration that licked up iron and glass as though they were among the combustibles. Neither can those who saw ever forget so spectacular an end. It seemed to herald Hitler's attack on England.

# 6

# Our Suffolk Inheritance

Sweet bird! thy bower is ever green,
Thy sky is ever clear:
Thou hast no sorrow in thy song,
No winter in thy year!
(*To the Cuckoo*—MICHAEL BRUCE
1746–1767)

Owing to the misfortune of my father's birth we had only two half-aunts on his side, so our whole outlook was to Mother's Suffolk. It was hardly ever out of our thoughts. It is a little difficult to convey what this meant to us living in a mean street, although it was far from being a bedraggled neighbourhood because we had Sydenham, Upper Norwood and Beckenham Village as neighbours. However, it gave us a green background. The fact remains, Suffolk, unspoilt Suffolk, was another world.

On looking back I realize that most of the fathers and mothers of the boys and girls I mixed with were of country origin, the result of the rural depopulation that had been going on for many years and came to a head about 1880; but not all were as favourably linked to a peaceful countryside as we were with our mother's country home in Suffolk. It was my fortune as a little boy that Mother used to visit her parents for three glorious weeks at cowslip time. What a wonderful first remembered journey that was. I have never been able to recapture the aura of that first time when I was not much more than three, remembering, of course, there can be only one first time. Although Mother had become a bit sophisticated to those Suffolk eyes, she remained a country woman at heart. She had not for-

66

gotten her days of girlhood, the life she lived, the simple pleasures. Every now and again would come out a little reminder in a rhyme of her youth and her face would light up,

> Bishop, bishop barnabee
> Tell me when my wedding be!

That for a ladybird that happened to light on one. Or—

> Good morrow, Walentine!
> Change yah luck as I do mine,
> We are raggetty, you are fine,
> So prah giv' us a Walentine.

A hopeful appeal for a penny rather than a rebuff.

It was a village steeped in history with a reach beyond the Domesday Book, dominated by a reed-thatched church, companioned by a thatched pub tucked away in a corner as though in disgrace, although it was named after a bell in the church tower; but with no squire to call its own. All the same everywhere was kept spick and span. A small river divided it from the next parish, so small that they gave it the name of Min and enlarged it to Minsmere when it got a little more water in it. It ambled on so quietly to the sea, with all sorts of queer little bits about it that we now call folklore. There was, for instance, a deep hole where a wagon and horses went in and were seen no more, and little venturesome boys, like myself, were warned not to go too near, otherwise they might be 'croomed' in (hooked), by some strange water sprite and be drowned. As I believed everything, it was effective. Then over the marshes ('maashes' to the locals), those willowy green marshes, was the sea, so that when a storm broke out and travelled eastward they used to say, "the sea ha' gort it", meaning the danger had passed. In the other direction, according to the wind, when you could hear those old blue engines whistling along, they said it was going to rain.

I never wanted to stray far from that old farmhouse and yard where my grandparents lived. The house, then divided into two dwellings, must have been one when Elizabeth I was queen. It all smelt so lovely, especially the little bit of an apple room where I slept on a feather bed on the floor, a room that was lit by a window just about as large as one in a period doll's house. You had to climb up a funny little staircase the entrance to which was a wall-papered door in the wall of the room below, and go through grandmother's bedroom to get to it. What annoyed me was that I slept so long in the morning, in spite of the fleas that seemed to be a part of country life, that half a lovely day was gone.

Sometimes Mother would go to the end of the farmyard where a gate led on to the marshes and at one particular spot the rushes grew. I can see them now. Her girlhood days would come back for a moment as she pleated them into a basket with a handle. Or she might twist poppies into dolls or soldiers, because the fields were full of them. Sometimes we would go down a lane called a drift, looking for flowers of which she knew the country names: harebells, mauve scabious, marsh marigolds. And it must be recalled that no one came home from a country holiday without a great bunch of flowers just to make the memory linger.

Those lovely fields were in full cultivation then and if we went a little later in the year they would be gold instead of green, spangled with flowers, especially poppies and the corn cockle. I must have been told on one occasion that out from one of the fields came our bread, so in boylike fashion, seeing grandfather at work there, I piped up, "Grandfather, can I come into the bread?" This caught on with the village youth and I never heard the last of it for years. It was reserved for a great occasion when we were allowed on Theberton Lawn to pick the cowslips but not the jonquils. There lived the Doughtys, a very nice, enlightened family, the ideal of squiredom.

The names of the farms seemed to suggest a picture of antiquity and of the configuration of the land, for instance Packway Farm, by the side of which the loaded pack-animals went silently on their journey. Fen Street Farm suggested a marshy boggy area, but Dove House Farm seemed screened in peace. Valley Farm was where Aunt Bessy lived who made such lovely buttercup butter, but you got the milk in a shiny tin can with a lid, from a little bit of a one-horsed farm kept by old Joe King. When he went to chapel he used to sit with his eyes closed, as if he was seeing visions. There was even a Water Mill Farm, but that was a bit out of our orbit; while Garden House Farm spoke for itself. Then, of course, keepers of inns were also farmers, such as Matthias Wright at 'The Bell', George Johnson at 'The Crown', Westleton or George Mills at 'The White Hart', Blythburgh. Smuggling might have been known at 'The Eels Foot' at East Bridge, but you could expect anything of a little inn tucked away in such a place. I wasn't old enough to enter into the romance of such a way of life and was scared rather than thrilled.

Also the countryside was haunted and you were made to feel it, especially with little bits of hidden nature overgrown with the years and names to match, such as Sarah Cobbler's pit. I didn't relish coming along the drift alone because it was so quiet and a bit eerie. I wasn't used to such utter loneliness after living in a crowded street. And as far as going about after dark, with a darkness that seemed to envelop one, that was too much. Even the natives were not given much that way, particularly if an old hoss happened to be wandering about loose. Moreover, there were sounds that travelled far, the barking of a dog or the shrill cry of despair of a rabbit caught in a trap.

If one went to other houses on a visit, especially after chapel on a Sunday afternoon, the curious thing was they all seemed much alike, with a grandfather clock in the corner, a grand-father chair near the fireplace and other bits and pieces that belonged to another century, especially the ornaments on the mantel-shelf. These were the occasions when you sampled Great Aunt Rebecca's rusks and lardy cakes or Cousin Rhoda's bread, but after all they weren't better than Grandmother's bakes, or the eggs which her chickens laid in all sorts of places. My seat at Aunt Rebecca's was a little four-legged stool, whose legs came out to the top. It had been made by Uncle Harry to rest Aunt's feet on and had been scrubbed white with wood ash until it shone.

Those old country roads had wide verges where there was enough feed for a horse or a cow, and one often saw someone attending such an animal getting a free meal. Moreover, those green borders added their charm to the scene with flowers, especially old man's beard and honeysuckle scenting the air, while the hedgerows were tall and straggling. Naturally when there was a drought they were covered with dust but that was an asset at harvest time.

Middleton had a rectory and there was something beautiful, almost cloistral about that creeper-mantled house that had one or two bricked-up windows reminiscent of the window tax. It suggested a green thought in a green shade, and one approached it quietly, sedately, whether coming from the village street and school, or better still from the beauty of Rackford Run. This was in reality its best and most secluded path, because you first came to Parson's Meadow where stood those lovely beech trees with their almost satin-like trunks and their spring and autumn beauty of foliage. In the paddock grew the largest and finest single snowdrops, which Grandmother knew all about as she was allowed to gather a few. In fact all sorts of blooms grew in all sorts of corners in that sheltered haven and matured garden.

The crescent-shaped drive was flanked by two iron gates, tribute to Garrett's of Leiston who made such things. Earlier rectors had looked rather splendid as they made their calls, but they may have gone to the 'arly sarvice' on foot when Pepper rang the tenor bell, but the ringers came into play for the eleven o'clock and those old bells went bim-bam to call the farmers and a few socially superior people who were not listed under tradesmen. It had been that way for many a long year when the poorest put on a bit of their best for the Sabbath.

The house had been built by a former curate who became rector in turn. He had travelled much abroad and had brought back that magnolia from Italy which still flourishes on the lawn before the creepered porch. It was probably he who had the stained-glass window installed on the staircase with a picture of Jerusalem and the inscription, *"In Amice Memoriam"*. Some have pondered as to who his friend could have been since no name is mentioned, but I wonder if this could have constituted an acknowledgement of the comfort he had received from that great hymn, "Jerusalem the golden, with milk and honey blest":

> O sweet and blessed country,
> The home of God's elect!
> O sweet and blessed Country
> That eager hearts expect!
> Jesu in mercy bring us
> To that dear land of rest;
> Who art with God the Father
> And Spirit ever blessed.

He died suddenly after preaching from the text, "Today shalt thou be with me in Paradise". I have an idea he might have dabbled in medicine and one likes to think of him brooding over the leaves of a herbal with his long fingers studying the properties of belladonna and arnica montana. When as a boy I went to that village the rector was a Scotsman with a voice under which no one could sleep. He preached for an hour and a half, so an hour-glass was of no use to him. It was said by those who knew that his first wife pined away and died because she was so lonely in that house of many rooms, and he buried her under an elaborate tomb. Later this preacher found another wife in a hotel where he was staying. She was a Scots lassie with a lovely voice that so charmed him that he took her back to that silent rectory.

It was said the rectory was haunted, so that one more ghost could be added to the list. This time it was a 'bachus' (backhouse) boy who pumped water from the pump in that outhouse at dead of night and persisted in opening the baize door that divided the house in two according to class, however fast closed it might have been.

The gardener-cum-coachman then was the father of two girls and a boy who lived the next field away from Grandmother's home. They were my first call on arrival when the holiday was still to be enjoyed. They were such a jolly lot. I have since discovered the relationship of this family which was contemporary with that of Mother's for some 150 years in that village. Susan took in washing, not just anyone's, but the pristine whiteness of the squire's family, which was delivered in hampers by a cockaded coachman. Her name before marriage was Pulham, that of a famous stud groom that appears in the first Stud Book of the Suffolk horse. He flourished in Middleton when a great-great grandfather was married there in 1799. During the course of time the two families intermarried, becoming Barham, and a daughter of Susan still survives.

How I loved it all. When the last day came I would go round and bid goodbye to this spot and that: the granary set above the cart shed where the meal cakes were stored and where the mice scampered away when the door was opened; the stackyard with its own chaffy smell, the barn loft where other food was stored and the horse pond to which the horses made their way and sucked up the water with a gentle suss-suss when the day was done. Do you wonder I shed some tears because next year seemed so far away? I would beg a few seeds of this and that to plant in our garden at home to remind me of those arcadian days. Of course they never came up.

Home again, that countryside was not forgotten, because a penny stamp would bring a wonderful letter. Grandfather, the kind old extrovert that he was, would conclude we could do with a taste of the old home. So, carefully tied up in a bit of sacking, sewn up with a packing needle, would come a piece of pork, butter, rusks, eggs, not forgetting a few flowers. This would be heralded by a postcard which cost a halfpenny, and to be sure to let him know we had received it safely. Even the old sacking smelt of the country and brought us visions of the little leaded light windows, the garden fence, the old flint wall and the pond around which the old 'hins' would lay their eggs making them difficult to find and the trees that screened it, the leaves of which were for ever rustling.

The countryside is still lovely, but its charm is not the same, nor can it ever be so endowed as in those years of yesterday. I am glad to have the memory of that old-world serenity that passed so slowly away.

The Suffolk directory states "Here is a Wesleyan chapel", which is rather a bald way of putting it, for as far as Grandfather was concerned, and his relations, it was the very hub of the village, and was full of memories and little happenings around those dear old folks that gathered there. It has altered but little since it came into being in 1828, a square-faced, square-built bit of Suffolk vernacular with a cap of red pantiles that you would under no circumstances mistake for a church. The front was, and is, lighted by a large window between two doors on the ground floor, three windows above and one on the south side; while the little forecourt is fenced in with iron railings. So far the outside.

When you enter by either door there is just a little space so that you can decide whether to take your seat with the faithful in the centre block or clatter up the bare wooden staircase that leads to a rare nice little Georgian gallery and gives a good view of the preacher and the singers on their raised platform facing one another. Needless to say, those stairs have to be taken into account on the ground floor, so a sort of alcove is provided at the sides. In the old days these were made cosy by two tortoise stoves with chimney pipes that got right hot and gave out a delicious heat. This had a rather soporific effect on a cold and windy night, and my word, it could blow at the chapel corner, as my old grandmother well knew. The advice was, "Don't git tew near, partner, or you'll be whooly scorched".

Those old stoves were like some members of the congregation —very temperamental and ruled by the wind. Sometimes they smoked and were wonderful slow to get a-going. Jonah Barham, of whom I have already written was the Sunday school superintendent and wore a kind smiling face. He had the bright idea one windy day when the stove looked as if it might give trouble, of going down on his hands and knees, opening the little door at the bottom and blowing right hard. Out came the soot and when he looked up, showing two fish eyes in a black face, Plumber Button who was with him exclaimed—"Whaa Jonah!" So he had to walk all the way home for a wash.

Now the chapel has had a great reputation for music and singing and when they came to organize the village band, nearly all the players were from the chapel. John Wesley when he died left behind a great legacy in a hymn-book of some 500 hymns, which for many a long year was known as the "Four-and-six-penny book", since that was its cost. This was used until the 1870s, when a committee discussed it and made it larger. It began with "O for a thousand tongues to sing" and ended with "Go on, we'll meet you there". Do you wonder they could sing long, short or common metre under such inspiration?

I don't suppose they had many copies of this book, because four-and-sixpence was a lot of money and not everyone could read. So the preacher, or minister, would not only give out the number but also read the first verse and the others in turn. As they were not versed in punctuation some rather strange effects were produced. One worthy man would persist in commencing with number 119: "Entering into my closet, I". This was not lost on those varmints of boys; and even poor old Charlie Chambers took a sly look at Joe Broom to see if he could make anything of it. Moreover, although there was such a choice of hymns, even the preachers would not have had a wider range than some sixteen. This was a pity because there were some very interesting specimens such as "Abraham, when severely tried", and "O my old, my bosom, foe". But there was also a wide range of the Psalms. When one of these modern American harmoniums was introduced, some of the old men thought it a dreadful box designed by Satan. They preferred the old tuning fork or their bit of an orchestra.

Perhaps it is invidious to poke fun at such a fine collection, but some of the opening lines suited their life so well. For example they would understand number 164, "Lord, regard my earnest cry; A potsherd of the earth". At least old Mrs Marjoram would have done, especially if one of her daughters, a grown woman, "brook a bason". She lived to be 100 and knew five generations of my family. She wore out my great grandmother's nightdress and her old tin candlestick. Then there was 368—"Father, see this living clod". Since they all lived by the land, that was quite understood. Number 180 went, "Saviour, I now with shame confess, My thirst for creature happiness". Poor old souls, they hadn't much of that, and if Grandmother when she grew old dreaded the wind and the cold, great-grandmother's possessions would have gone into a wheelbarrow. Sometimes 310, "Into a world of ruffians sent", seemed to sum up some of their neighbours.

Someone, somewhen, introduced a very shiny-faced clock, which was placed plumb in the middle of the gallery facing the preacher. That was all very well and much better than the old hour-glass in the church. Besides, it had a loud tick. Alas, it became a target for those rascals of boys, who by some means or other fiddled the hands so that time went a bit faster. This caused old John Newstead to give a short exordium on the verb "to do". He approached Charlie Godward (Goddard in local parlance): "Yew'll het-a dew suffen about that there clock, Charlie. Them thare bors ar' a interfering wi tha works". So Charlie had the blarmed thing boxed in.

Just another little bit about old John. A special meeting had been arranged in Ipswich and several members of Middleton chapel went to it. They all got on a trolley-bus and when the conductor said to John, "Where to?" he replied, "I doan't fare to know, you'll hett a ask Mrs Tairga!" (Teager). And one other sample of natural humour: half-way up the little rise that leads to the turnpike, just to the left lived a couple in a very small hut with only one door. Mrs Mulley took in washing and a villager for whom she worked had occasion to send her old father with a message. He knocked on the door which was opened by Mulley himself. "Excuse me a' comin' tew tha *front* door, Bob", was his polite bit of introduction. This brought the reply, "Thass all right, George, thass all right!"

Going back to the church. You should know that that's whooly old. It seems a bit funny they put the two churches in one acre of ground. However, all paths led thither. One has just been done away with, the hedge has been taken up and there is no path. According to oral tradition it led from the moor by Hulver Hill and Hogweed Lane (what lovely old names) to the church. It was wide enough for two to walk abreast for funerals. If for the latter, then also for those old walking weddings, when Grandmother wore her best sprigged gown, possibly made by her sister, who was also her aunt by marriage. How pretty she must have looked under a blue and white sky on her wedding day, with the sun fairly dancing on her dappled way. After all, she couldn't get married in chapel in those days. And it was for life.

> 'The ring so worn, as you behold,
> So thin, so pale, is yet of gold:
> The passion such it was to prove;
> Worn with life's cares, love yet was love.'
>
> GEORGE CRABBE

# 7

# Bagshot

<br>

I doubt if there be any scene in the world more animating or delightful than a cricket match.

MARY RUSSELL MITFORD

Suffolk was not the only link with the countryside that we as suburbanites possessed, but it was by far the strongest. Our father had a half-sister living at Bagshot in Surrey, of whom he was very fond and she of him. Indeed, he had been something of a guardian to her when her mother died. She had followed him to Penge and had been married at St John's Church. They were quite a jolly family of two boys and two girls. One of the boys was always pulling my leg about the treacle mines at Chobham. We did not often go there *en famille* and my own visits were not made until I had grown up into young manhood, but they were sufficient to stimulate a love and appreciation for this romantic old township on the then Portsmouth and Southampton roads.

But how different it all was from that simple unknown Suffolk village. It was more sophisticated with its flavour of stage-coaches, highway robbery, and cricket; and behind it spreading like a purple mantle, the regal splendour of Windsor. There was another contrast, for whereas Grandfather was a chapel-goer, there our aunt and uncle were church folk and he a verger at the neo-Gothic church with its delicate and slender spire. It was only natural therefore that we went to church and that life and conversation centred about the establishment.

The church was built in a corner of Bagshot Park, the real

home of the Duke of Connaught, and when at home he was a never-failing member of the congregation; walking across the Park and entering by a north door to take his place in the pews, furnished in blue, reserved for himself and his guests. A frequent visitor was the then Crown Prince of Sweden, later king, and his daughter the youthful Princess Ingrid; he a tall soldierly figure, she a young girl. Creed and politics counted for nothing, anyone in the house party came, including his Catholic Majesty, King Alfonso of Spain. I was in that congregation when the dignified, bent figure of the Duke moved across to the north wall to unveil a tablet to the memory of his wife, a Princess of Prussia and his daughter, the Crown Princess of Sweden whose early death was so sore a blow to a very united family.

We sat at the back of this very full and fashionable church, and beside the great west window dedicated to Queen Victoria were two two-light windows at the end of the two aisles. These were filled by angelic creatures, being actual portraits of an old general's relatives, those at the end of the south aisle of his father and mother and at the north aisle of two former wives who had died very young at foreign stations. I thought these two latter very beautiful, especially one who was only eighteen when she died in Malta. The old man had a pew immediately below these two sad and pensive portraits, and would come in with his third wife to take part in the midday communion. He looked much like Wellington, with his aquiline nose and would sit there quiet and dignified and those angelic faces appeared to look down with surprise at the ageing form of their one-time spouse who had looked so magnifical as a Captain of Engineers.

Another interesting worshipper there associated with the ducal pew and coming from a house situated in the pine woods was the widow of Sir Howard Elphingstone who had been tragically lost at sea when on a voyage of recuperation for his health. She had married him, a middle-aged man, when she was but a girl and through him was a direct link with the Crimea and the Indian Mutiny. She would creep down the south aisle to sit near her husband's splendid memorial of window and brass. Yet another on visiting terms with the head of the blue decorated pews was a Miss Cave, a member of a famous banking family. She had been a fine horsewoman in her time and was a lover of music who maintained an amateur orchestra in her house. She had been my uncle's employer when she lived at the Green Farm and when he, a gardener, and his family lived in a lowly shed-like tin house, then thought sufficient guerdon for retainers.

Bagshot was full of old inns evoking battle honours and battles not so long ago. It is said there were twenty-six public houses in the village in the sixties of last century, obviously a reminder of its proximity to Aldershot. These included 'The Hit and Miss', 'Luck is All' and 'The Hero of Inkerman', 'The Fighting Cocks', 'Kings Arms', 'Half Moon', 'Three Mariners' and 'The White Hart'. It was at the latter that Queen Victoria used to stop to change horses when on her way from Windsor to Farnborough station going to Osborne House. Bagshot was a long straggling village and possessed the picturesque Regency-flavoured inn dedicated to the Cricketers at its northern extremity and 'The Jolly Farmer' on the south, the latter romantic by its supposed association with Dick Turpin and his exploits on Bagshot Heath.

Then there was a collection of old country shops clustering about the square, with a vivid reminder of the Industrial Revolution in the fine though somewhat gaunt viaduct carrying the branch line from Ascot to Woking. That line led to the blue haze of Farnborough, where in the kaleidoscope of history set on a hill within a bit of France is the mausoleum of the last of the Napoleons, the child of France with his father and mother; held high in the walls, embalming the blundering, cowardly incident of the kraal of Etuki in the Zulu War.

Not far away was Eversley and the grave of Charles Kingsley with its Latin conjugations of the verb 'to love'. His eroticism has strangely come to light in these recent years and another unknown personality exposed to view.

Bagshot was and is famed for its nurseries and the time to visit it is when the rhododendrons glow magenta and azaleas spread their glory. The sandy soil so beloved by conifers produces their shades to perfection, as also in nearby Windsor Great Park. When the nurseries were thrown open to the public it was a great treat to be able to walk about their ways amid this display of living colour. Then too, at blossom time came the spectacle of Ascot, featuring the Ladies' Mile and petals of another culture. Broom-making was associated with Bagshot and there used to be such a place as 'Hockley's Broom Kiln up Potato Row'. And I used to watch the sun-dew in bloom with its insect-laden petals at Lightwater Marsh.

Father, who was so very fond of fishing, got up early one morning to practise at Rapley Lake, when he thought he espied a keeper. His speedy exit was a remarkable bit of vaulting on his crutch.

There were also in Bagshot some of the most picturesque characters I have ever met. At the Green Farm lived and worked two sisters, the most queer and distinctive of their kind. They did the work of men, were inseparable and lived much like the cattle they tended. One was Tot and the other Liz, both with full-moon faces, one high-pitched and the other deep and masculine in tone. They tramped about with their skirts tucked up, understood their charges as a mother a child, were kindness itself and as companionable to others as to one another. Memory of them is of their oddness—not the less pleasant because of their Saxon serf-like appearance and way of life.

Two other picturesque characters lived in a real Squatter's Hut, built of turves and bracken, then to be found on Barossa Common, and undoubtedly the last of its kind in this country. Two old folks lived in this house of their own fashioning, behind bottle-bleb windows and beneath a lowly roof. They tended the bit of garden they had cleared of heather and ling. Alas, local

The Finished Overmantel, 1887

(Courtesy of *The Lady*)

Myself before going off to France

agitated authorities swept them away, leaving not a wrack behind, and in so doing destroyed this link with elves and fairies
living on into a wicked world.

Near High Curly, a sandy prominence, lived an old woman
who cured warts by charming them away. She amused the vicar,
when he called, by complaining she had bushes (thorns) in her
feet.

Later, Aunt and Uncle moved to an old Queen Anne house
which had been the first vicarage, named the Red House. This
provided a front seat when George V and his sons passed the
door on their way to the Army Cup Final at Aldershot.

Another memory was a visit to the Farnborough flying ground
to see the early aeroplanes not reckoning one whit the significance
those machines were to have in war and upon our civilization.
Yet we had seen one of the earliest, piloted by Wilbur Wright
making its way to the Crystal Palace, just above our chimney
pots. As also that 'Cowboy of the Skies', Col. Cody, manipulat-
ing his man-lifting kites in the Palace grounds. He was to be
the first to make a successful flight in Great Britain, at Farnborough.

One thing more, Bagshot possesses (still, I hope), one of the
best and longest holly-hedges to be found anywhere. It sur-
rounds Penny Hill Park. At one part on the church side it rises
to a very great height.

Country holidays, enjoyed almost as much by anticipation,
ended with almost tragic swiftness. I always associate Bagshot
with French marigolds that grew there in great profusion. Also
the little streams and the water butts were full of darting water
beetles, not found in Suffolk.

# 8

# Church and Sunday School

---

If to do were as easy as to know what to do, chapels had been churches, and poor men's cottages princes' palaces.

SHAKESPEARE

Both my parents came of good Methodist stock and were deeply religious. The fervour of the last two decades of the nineteenth century affected them greatly, so that names like Moody and Sankey, with that of Spurgeon, were household words with us. Indeed, religion and its great controversies were taken seriously then and people got very hot about things which, today, would pass unnoticed. For example, Colenso, Bishop of Natal, caused a great stir with his criticism of the Pentateuch and the naïve statement that he couldn't see how all those animals could have got into the Ark. Then there was the famous Gorham Case, which revolved around Baptismal regeneration, and the unknowable election or rejection of the individual soul.

As a family we had nothing material to gain by this religious profession, save in the uplift that it gave. What our home and outlook would have been without it I cannot say. But remembering where we lived, the little my father earned, and our close proximity to the seamy side of life, there is little doubt that we should have joined the great unwashed. It was our mother who kept us all on the upgrade. Religion was a dynamic reality with her and shed a light on a very humdrum existence. George Herbert had a word for it,

> Let thy mind's sweetness have its operation
> Upon thy person, clothes and habitation.

The effect of a religious outlook was shown in Father's workshop window-blind, which was lowered every Saturday night and not pulled up again until Monday morning. The window only gave out on to our little back yard. This small gesture had something fine in it and needs no embellishment from me.

Our church was over the bridge, almost in a line with our house on the other side of the railway. It was an imposing building in the neo-Gothic style, with a truncated tower designed for a spire. It could not have been very old when I was born, but as it was ivy-clad and built of Kentish rag, it took on the semblance of age. The original small chapel, having passed the tin-roofed stage, had become the Sunday school, the two buildings providing plenty of accommodation. Curiously enough, the elaborate, spireless building disappeared in the bombing of London, and no one seemed to lament its passing, certainly not the trustees, for it had become a problem. But the bit of Carpenter's Gothic behind it survived and the Methodist Society has returned to first thing.

Methodists of my youth spoke of our church as a cathedral, and it certainly was a noble excursion in non-conformist building, for it was provided with a central aisle and transepts. It also had what was a *sine qua non* in those days, a huge gallery, so that the place would seat a thousand. The old Methodists always looked towards an advance, although their vision proved too optimistic. Inside the building pitch-pine dominated the scene, with a great expanse of roof, the vast arrangement of pews, supplemented by the three galleries, all decked out in varnish. The pillars that support the galleries were grained to simulate marble (but so were the pilasters of our pub) and had Corinthian capitals. In the old days it was lit by gas, its aisles were covered with coco-matting, and its many windows shed a cold light through opaque glass. The dominating feature, symbolizing the central act of all the services, was the pulpit, set so as to obscure the communion table. That too was of pine, a veritable triumph of the carpenter's workshop. This, then, was the chapel that ruled and ordered our whole life.

I must have been a very tiny boy when I first became conscious of the people who formed the congregation. I can see them now as I sat in the pew that had become ours by adoption, making their way along those aisles to their favourite places. Some were old, very old, and the family element loomed large and some had pock-marked faces, then quite a common sight. Many of them could point to the day, hour and spot when and where they were converted. Generally speaking they were simple un-ostentatious folk of the working class, although a few were exceedingly magnificent in attire and demeanour, whose progress along the central aisle was worth watching.

It was an age of long sermons and expository preaching, so that one did not escape under an hour and a half. But the time was always redeemed by Wesley's hymns, which were chosen with great care and sung with great effect. If John bequeathed fifty-three sermons as a mandatory charge on his student successors, he and Charles provided them with a lyric for every occasion, as sound in theology as in meter. No collection of hymns has ever excelled in quality and force that belonging to, and inherited by, the "People Called Methodists".

Sunday was a full day with us, morning service at eleven, which was liturgical, Sunday school in the afternoon and service again at night, with at the latter very often an 'after meeting'. And, strange as it may seem, there was a ritual in those services, without which they would have fallen to pieces. For example, at the morning service, the chapel-keeper would cross from the vestry walking softly and carrying a Bible and prayer book which he would place on the reading desk, the slope of which was decorated with a fringed cloth. This done, he would return for another and even larger Bible, with which he would climb the winding stairs of the pulpit and most reverently place it on a similar beclothed and fringed slope. The choir in place, the minister would emerge from that same hidden vestry, attired in solemn clothes, and the first hymn would be announced. The whole progress of prayers and psalms, creed and readings was towards the sermon, which varied according to the inspiration or lack of it, in the man concerned. How often have I listened to those long and weary discourses, watching the play of light in the chancel window, which had a little colour in it. The gable of the old schoolroom cast a shadow across the arch, the angle of which grew longer and wider as the discourse drew to its dreary close.

When a church member died, the crimson cloth on the reading desk and the pulpit turned to black, and the Dead March in *Saul* was played. I can hear now those awful rumblings and groans, that I thought were being made by the deceased, whom perchance I had seen alive and well, sitting in one of those pews, and was now on the way to heaven just above that pitch-pine roof.

I may be wrong, but I always looked upon those devoted servants of that old chapel as godly men and women. I believe the chapel-keeper was a saint, harassed and chivied by many masters, yet a saint. I can remember him tinkering about with the gas taps that were set in an alcove just behind the 'free seats' where we sat. And there was another, a house painter, who prayed with such fervour as to leave no time for other suppliants. He with others, might have been heard punctuating a sermon or a prayer with notes of appreciation and approval. By and large, rich and poor, they were to us all Fathers in Israel—workers for the Church—and their memory is fragrant.

We had one Judas, however, a small sandy-haired man who was I think the church secretary. He had an oil and colour business in the Station Road. He was also secretary to the Penge Provident Building Society. One day the alarming news got about that he had milked the latter of every penny. It broke many a poor man's heart whose life savings had gone and shook our church to its very foundations. I believe he had some of the chapel funds as well. The worst part was that he was the son of one of the founders of the church with a memorial tablet on the walls facing the congregation.

Then there were the women folk, who, dressed as they were in those days in dark clothes made to last, appeared old when they were quite young. There was one old lady, a minister's widow, who always wore black with white, with side curls, that spoke of an even earlier fashion. She was carefully screened by her daughters who treated her with such loving care that nothing of disaster or trouble came to her knowledge. Her pleasant, smiling, nodding face looked out on a world of make-believe.

And there was the usual sprinkling of those domineering authoritative, almost terrifying women, so numerous in those days. They were class leaders, Mothers In Israel it is true, and they did a lot of good. They seemed to rule the approaches to the mission field, presided over sewing meetings, led various girls' and women's classes, and acted as the power behind the throne. They certainly filled a great place in Methodism, as they did in many other spheres of life.

Sometimes after the evening service there would be a prayer meeting, particularly if hearts had been touched during the sermon. Or there might be a love feast, a meeting, I believe, peculiar to Methodism, but of a very ancient origin. I can remember the two-handled mug of water being handed round and a biscuit in a basket. Just as the C. of E. has its Communion plate, so Methodism had its holy vessels. These consisted of a white and gold ewer, basin and dish, bearing the words in gold— 'Penge Wesleyan Methodist Chapel'. Needless to say, both the fervour and the love feast have completely passed away.

There were two lines of ambition nourished deep in the hearts of Methodist mothers. One was that a son might become a minister, or failing that an office-bearer in the church. They were worthy desires, for those old ministers were rightly held in great esteem, for in such a church as Methodism there were no sinecures. Moreover, the Church as a body was wholesomely free of political bias, although of course its outlook was more

Liberal than otherwise. Again the triennial system was another touch of genius, with the first Sunday in September becoming in the nature of an unknown quantity when the new ministers in the circuit appeared in the pulpit for the first time, and all their peculiarities came under scrutiny. So that each year, as in a great school, there was a *Valete* as well as a *Salvete*.

Another service peculiar to Methodism was held on the first Sunday afternoon of the New Year. It was the Covenant Service, and then it was that one was made to feel one's membership of the family, because a roll was called, each man and woman having his or her name read out in full. The service, provided for in the Methodist Prayer Book, concluded with the Lord's Supper. Just as the New Year was ushered in with the Watch-night Service, and the singing of that peculiar excursion into hymnody—"Come let us anew our journey pursue", so the Covenant Service confirmed the work of grace.

Membership of the church was only achieved by membership of a society class, to give it its correct designation. The Class system was really the genius of the constitution in spite of what Howard Spring said about it, and for many years it was the main source of revenue. Naturally a lot depended on the leaders, men and women much above their fellows in acumen and wisdom. The members would gather round them once a week, sing the old hymns, pray and give their testimony. It must be remembered that Methodist people always seemed to have an experience worth relating. It was a wonderful institution for knitting the various age groups together and keeping them interested. Then once a quarter the minister would meet the Class for tickets of membership, which were little white billets bearing a letter of the alphabet, a verse of scripture, and the recipient's name written in full and signed with the minister's initials. Old Methodists were very jealous in collecting these little tokens, and many a bundle covering long years of life, tied up with tape have gone down into the grave when the end came.

It is not without significance that two writers outside the

Methodist Church and somewhat removed from one another in outlook, have spoken of this unique institution of the Class Meeting. One, a Roman Catholic, said, "To the outsider the disappearance of the regular Class Meetings as a normal part of Methodism looks almost like a fatal occurrence."

The other was Canon E. R. Wickham (now Bishop Suffragan of Middleton) in his book, *Church and People in an Industrial City*. He said, "In fact the Class Meetings became the strong ground-floor structure of the Methodist Societies, accomplishing ends that were never envisaged—not only religious and pastoral, but also creating vital centres of responsible community life. They produced an active and articulate laity such as no other denomination has produced, not only within the Connexion but in secular society . . . Wesley was right."

Naturally I became a member of one of these classes, one devoted to young men. It was led by a bachelor who had literally made it his life's work and calling. He was a civil servant, and had deliberately retarded his progress so that he might continue to lead his youthful band. He was a man of no education, musical, with a nice taste in hymns, and was guided through life by the uncertain light of common sense. For example, a prolix brother arriving at his turn to tell his tale, and not knowing where to start, would be enjoined to "begin near the end".

We used to meet in an upper vestry, sit round a table on bentwood chairs that rattled, and kneel to pray. In the room below, the fathers met and our devotions plus our lusty efforts at singing, drove them into an involuntary silence. Sad to relate, those chairs emptied as the First World War waged its weary way of attrition, and so many of those fine, clean, gay young fellows went down those stairs for the last time, falling victims to a hide-bound, purblind military staff who had been cast in a mould that believed war was a gentleman's job. I do not think the Methodist Church ever recovered from that loss of youth.

Our Sunday school was a wonderful institution but I went to it reluctantly and tearfully at a very early age. It was our

Mother who attended to all disciplinary affairs, because Father was lame and soft-hearted at that, and it was she who saw to it that I went. I remember dawdling over our railway bridge, weeping, but all to no purpose. I had to go. What did I find there? Well, we were gathered together in a large room known as the church parlour, and sat on bentwood chairs that seemed a long way from the floor, round a large dining table. The hymn we were taught to lisp was, "Shall we gather at the River?" I was not very old but I knew what it meant and had not the least desire to do any such thing. I was always haunted by two dead children whom I had never seen, a brother and sister. Besides, the little white coffins that passed our window all too often were enough for me. The redeeming feature of the proceedings was a teacher, a very nice-looking young woman, destined soon to be the wife of a minister. In my childish ruminations I thought he was lucky. Perhaps I grew out of, or became accustomed to that school and the hymns, for I got to like it and stayed on until I was a young man.

The main school was a large building with leaded-light windows, two transepts and a rostrum that went across the top of the room, under a window that should have borne the name of rose, but was in fact like a circular case of scissors. I have often watched the shadows creeping past it towards the west. Then, as a companion to the church parlour was a little whitewashed chamber room known as the sepulchre. Boys went up the left-hand side as far as the transept (these could be converted into classrooms by means of red curtains with a *fleur-de-lis* design), and the girls similarly on the right, with the centre forms catering for both sexes.

Our superintendent was a great personality, a Manchester merchant. He was immaculate and more than visible, with frock coat, striped trousers and fancy waistcoat, all *de rigueur*, and his cravat was held in place by a gold ring. He had a fine bifurcated beard that came down like two fangs; and when he was a bit rattled he would pull at these two appendages as though milking a cow. He wore gold spectacles that seemed to sparkle and illuminate his sandy face.

We all knelt to pray and our superintendent did likewise, but whereas we knelt on the bare floor, he knelt on the rostrum; before doing so he pulled out a spotless white handkerchief to shield his trousers. I have often thought about that old leader, so high above us, reminding us so often that he was a J.P. and that if we didn't behave ourselves we should find ourselves before him in the little red house across the way. But I have come to the conclusion that he belonged of right to that select band spoken of in the *Benedicite* as "Holy and humble men of heart". Why else should he have deprived himself of his post-prandial nap and interested himself in our raggle-taggle band?

I moved up that school from just behind the church parlour door. Two or three classes on, there was a large stone let into the floor, on which an ancient stove shed its ashes. Considering we were bare-kneed in knickerbockers our devotions took on the savour of a penance, and we longed for the next move.

Our school year was punctuated by one great festival, and that was the anniversary. For that we were handed over to a singing master. Poor man, how he perspired, and so did we. He led us up and down the scale until we knew it all by rote. Then, on the great Sunday, we were ushered into the chancel of the church, sat on forms or chairs, and did our best. That was our tutor's reward for his pains and labours. If we were lucky we might get a seat next the preacher himself, who, once during the reign of our Manchester superintendent was an eminent lay scientist, a Doctor Dallinger. I even remember his text, "Consider the lilies of the field".

Monday evening saw our prize-giving, which was held in the school room. It was attended by a motley down-town audience who never at any other time darkened the doors of our, or any other sanctuary. Again we sang and said our pieces. Once I was foolish enough to embark on "The Burial of Sir John Moore", and nearly died of fright. The prizes given and received, we started on another year.

By the time we had reached the transepts we were young men and women. The two classes that faced one another across the arid waste of rostrum were led by two brothers. Our own was the bachelor class leader, while that of the young women was the father of a family. As our man was allergic to women, no glances were allowed towards the sisterhood, although some were worth a look. Indeed, it might be mentioned that two girls attending the School at Upper Norwood were Phyllis and Zena Dare, but they were not within our view.

Our old superintendent had two favourite hymns. One was used at the opening:

> I thank the goodness and the grace
> Which on my birth have smiled,
> And made me, in these Christian days,
> A happy English child.
>
> JANE TAYLOR

At his request we substituted "British" for "English", evidently having in mind the Empire status to which we had attained.

The other was a dismissal hymn, which I used to think was a bit melancholy, but it was typical of those dear dead days. It was the lovely and rather plaintive:

> Holy Father cheer our way!
> With Thy love's perpetual ray;
> Grant us every closing day
> Light at evening time.

I wonder if soft echoes of that last verse caressed those fair youths as they lay dying in Flanders' mud:

> Holy, Blessed Trinity!
> Darkness is not dark with Thee;
> Those Thou keepest always see
> Light at evening time.

# 9

# Slate Pencil Days

---



I have to confess to at least two incurable habits. One is that of looking out of railway carriage windows, and the other of wandering in churchyards and cemeteries. When I go back to my native bit of south-east London, I never feel the visit complete unless I can find time to go down the hill to that now crowded Elmers End. Why? Partly because my mother and father lie there, but chiefly because I know more people there than anywhere else. I wander along those avenues, lined so thickly, scan this name and that, and am back in the days of my youth, when so many of those men and women were alive and formed my world.

> Now a very little girth
> Holds what once the earth
> Seemed too narrow to contain.

Under the trees, waiting for his next innings, lies England's greatest cricketer, and not far removed our local doctor, once so magnifical in person and calling. Over there, gathered into an enclave all their own, with a tall slender Saxon cross covering their shepherd, lie the worshippers at our one and only High Church, still following in solemn files their vicar who was of large proportions and who exercised the male privilege of being ugly. Then, still keeping to the 'Church' side, for even in death our dead are divided, lie two graves not far from one

another that are of especial interest to me. One is that of the
Vicar of Penge, to whose school I eventually drifted; the other
is that of the headmaster.

My very early years were spent at a dame's school, and
although I stayed under that sort of influence too long, I look
back with thankfulness that my mother was thrifty enough and
scraped together a shilling a week, which was the fee. A shilling
in those days was a lot of money for poor people. I remember
the consternation when I managed to lose it one week.

The first of these schools was one my brother had attended
before me, kept by a Mrs Reuill, pronounced most appropriately
'Rule'. It was a queer academy and I cannot remember ever
having seen the lady in question. As far as I was concerned she
was like Queen Victoria in a play, always off-stage. She had one
or two pupil teachers who did the work, which was but a pre-
tence at teaching, and I was given small sums to do yet never
instructed as to how they might produce an answer. When my
brother went there it was housed in Anerley Station Road, in a
public hall that never functioned as such, but became a printing
press for our local paper. Opposite was one of those ladies' repositories that sold papers and magazines, the latter at a dis-
count of twenty-five per cent, a practice then common. Mrs
Reuill must have had some sort of agreement with the Baptist
spinsters who ran it, because at the latter part of the week, she
would send across to collect the latest issues, which having
read, would be returned. I also understand that if she was not
visible she could be heard, giving instructions in a loud voice.
She died before I had been there many weeks, and I was glad.
Presumably the male Reuill had been folded up and put away
long before.

My next school was another such academy, with mostly little
girls as pupils—to me who had no sister, quite lovely; there
were also one or two little boys. One of these latter has always
remained in my memory because he had what was even then
not very common, long ringlet curls. How they did stink! I

have always been allergic to smells and I remember that little boy's hair. He would persist in sitting near me. An afternoon diversion was being read to from the unbound parts of a magazine, and I think the tale was *Queechy*. I gave no trouble on those occasions. I don't suppose I learned much there, but I gained perhaps a little sadly needed polish. Once a year we had a party, were admitted into the sanctity of the room upstairs where was the piano, and where the favoured few at sixpence per week extra took their music lessons. I remember how thoroughly my mother scrubbed me up for this wonderful treat of tea and games.

My next move came about through a friendship made with a little bright boy whom I met at Sunday school. It was to a church school of great local repute. I remember how he came to our house and persuaded Mother to let me go to his school. He was to become quite an eminent ophthalmologist. As something had to be done, she must have agreed, because my father, by appointment, took me along for an interview with the headmaster. I remember it all so well, making our way across the silent playground to the main door, and being ushered into a little room on the right. How long it took I can't recall, but I remember one question the great man asked me, "What does your mother call your father?" My IQ couldn't have been very high because I was floored. Father's name was Edward and she called him Ted. One thing, however, I do remember, he reminded my father that we lived in a road with a bad reputation, but as we were Methodists, and he had several good Methodists there, he would take me.

The school was living on a great reputation bequeathed to it by a headmaster who died just before I got there. He must have been a great personality, because he had imprinted his own name on the institution. It was really St John's Boys' School, Penge, housed in what must have been the first proprietary chapel in the hamlet of Penge, erected in 1837 as a breakaway from Beckenham. It was almost a charity belonging to the parish church, but to all and sundry, it was proudly known as 'Cook's School'. In my time it was ruled over by one of his bright boys, but evidently one not possessing as great a personality, and was staffed by men, most of them middle-aged and uncertificated. As far as I can remember the classes comprised some fifty or sixty boys. Each class was in a separate room, some cubicles being formed by sliding screens, and some rooms had tiers for the back seats.

The fee was a penny a day, the same you may remember as that paid to the labourers in the vineyard, and this was payable on a Monday morning. I remember those little piles of coppers, collected together on a slate and placed on the master's desk. Later it was rounded off to sixpence a week.

It had been customary at the mother church to preach sermons once a year for certain charitable objects, notably the schools attached to itself and the nearby Royal Asylum for Watermen. And this is the sort of thing that touched the hearts and pockets of the local fathers. In the annual sermon appealing for funds the preacher described it as one of the best things they could possibly give to. It provided rest for the aged—they knew it—could see it—it was in their midst—it provided a respectable home "for the poor from whom God has thought fit to withhold riches".

And this was the outcry for the schools (there was also one for girls—which as an infants school, still survives.) "And now brethren, what will you say when I tell you that this morning the miserable sum of £15 only was given as a result of the appeal from this pulpit? I could almost say it with tears that the people of this locality could make such an offering to the schools which are doing so great a work. We depend upon this source of income to maintain the schools, upon the Government grant which we earn, the children's pence (one penny a day), and upon voluntary subscriptions from the parishioners. The Board Schools have no difficulty whatever. Would you like us to hand over our schools? . . . If we cannot compare with the best Board

Schools, shut us up! If we are not efficient, shut us up! And if we do not contrast favourably with a large number of Board Schools, I say shut us up!" The preacher anticipated events by about fifty years.

We commenced each day with a hymn, sung by the assembled school, which might be:

> Jesus high in glory,
> Lend a listening ear—

Or,

> Day by day we magnify Thee,
> When our hymns in school we raise,
> Daily work begun and ended
> With the daily voice of praise.

Now that I am grown old I never come to the phrase in the *Te Deum* without being carried back to those sunlit mornings, and hearing afresh those treble voices, of which mine was one, declaiming sentiments we never knew. Each dawning then was indeed a New Day.

The hymn would be followed by a Collect, and if the school did no more, it introduced me to Cranmer's English. Sometimes our Scripture lessons were taken by the curate, an earnest young Irishman. I remember the roll of his voice and the beads of perspiration that stood out on his forehead. Then, once a week or month, we had the Catechism, which to me was the greatest of enigmas. "What is your name?" "Who gave you that name?" I thought everyone connected with us knew without asking. However, there was one great advantage in belonging to that school and that was each Ash Wednesday and Ascension Day, as they came round, saw us being marched off to the church in the morning, with a holiday in the afternoon. But when we were at lessons how slowly crept those clock hands towards the hour that let us live. And even then we had homework.

Our vicar was an Irishman, hence the curate, one of the

The first of the family

Passing the Parthenon

numerous sons of that island, who left it as soon as possible to fill up the ranks of the church, the army, the medical and legal professions. He wore a little white necktie over a clerical cut of waistcoat, and walked about head foremost with his coat-tails flying in the breeze of his own creation. Occasionally he would burst into our class room, unheralded, with "Good morning boys!" To this we would reply, stampeding to our feet with, "Good morning, sir!"

The curriculum could not have been of a very high order, perhaps one could not expect too much of those masters at that fee. Yet there was an Honours Board, if not two of them. I remember gazing with awe at those names which meant so little to me. I knew then that my name would never be added to the list. But what I do remember very distinctly was that the older boys seemed so grown up and far above me. Perhaps that was natural, because the school consisted of two grades, Upper and Lower. Soon after I joined, the Beckenham Technical Institute opened, and the Upper Grade disappeared to that academy.

Emphases were laid on things far beyond me. One of these was writing, that essential qualification for a clerkship before the universal use of typewriters, now done by women. Mine was atrocious and messy, a study in blots, smudges, and generally indecipherable. But we might recall the delectable words of the old Catechism, "To learn and labour truly to get mine own living, and to do my duty in that state of life unto which it shall please God to call me". Then we were instructed in some elementary form of book-keeping, even rising to what was known as double entry.

Slates were then in daily use, and we used those noisy and noisome things, rattling them into and out of our desks, scratching away with slate pencils. We cleaned them as all the generations before us, with a little humid breath, or that natural asset provided for a boy's various needs—a little spit.

I was at that school when Queen Victoria died, and I can

recall so well being assembled together to hear the headmaster dilate on that wonderful reign and the heritage into which we had entered since 1837. It is curious to realize how far away and long ago it all was. But we were far nearer to that year of accession then, than we are to her passing now. We were reminded of the coming of the railways, telegraphs, telephones, but above all of the doctrines of security and international brotherhood, of which our Crystal Palace was but the flowering. So much had been achieved in those long years of her reign that appeared so changeless. When the new reign was on its way, we had a day at the Palace and were given a tin medal and a mug. And that was that.

We learned part-singing, which was natural because the head and some of the assistant masters were in the church choir. But as my part was only flat I did not shine even at that. Then some verses were committed to memory, of which the "Lays of Ancient Rome" took a prominent part. I remember one poor wight who got the "highest turret tops", mixed up with "turnip tops", to the scornful derision of the master and my unbounded satisfaction. One lay, however, was to prove strangely prophetic to us of that generation, which we lisped unheedingly:

> And Ardennes waves above them her green leaves,
> Dewy with Nature's tear-drops, as they pass,
> Grieving, if aught inanimate e'er grieves,
> Over the unreturning brave,—alas!
> Ere evening to be trodden like the grass,
> Which *now* beneath them, but *above* shall grow
> In its next verdure . . .
>
> BYRON

When paying attention to our master's oracular statements, since we were under the instruction of one man for all the subjects, except scripture, we sat at those old iron-framed, ink-bespattered desks with our arms folded. And we gazed in mute astonishment that one small head could contain all he knew. Then, as occasion required, we received four handers (or less or more) with heroic stoicism, and were dismissed with that lovely hymn, piped in full throated unison:

> Saviour, again to Thy dear name we raise
> With one accord our parting hymn of praise;
> We stand to bless Thee ere our worship cease,
> Then lowly kneeling, wait Thy word of peace.

At the close of the school year there was a general assembly and prizes were distributed. I remember sitting there somewhere at the back, watching the others walk up for their rewards. Needless to say, there were none for me. Those heights were far beyond my scaling. Summer holidays then were four whole weeks, which I used to think was an enormous period of time. And so it was when the working days were so long and the hours of play so short.

The place of our school is no more. Gone are the pseudo-Gothic windows, the paved yard, the Honours Boards, the bell, the books, the birch. In its place are certain multiple shops, streamlined in chromium with neon lighting. Meanwhile the electronic guitar plays on.

# 10

# The Changing Sky

"Where the goat is tied there she must browse".

The best time of one's life came inevitably to an end, in my case abruptly and unexpectedly. I was coming home from school with other boys when we lingered over the swings in the Penge recreation ground. Somehow or other I got in the way and received the full force of a loaded swing just over my left eye. It was providential that it missed the eyeball and my sight was unimpaired. As I was fourteen with a nasty wound I never returned to those desks, the old schoolyard and a tutorial system that would have left me undone and ignorant even if I had stayed on indefinitely. I never reached the seventh standard. However, if I left something which was no great joy I was landed in something infinitely worse.

School over, the one concern was that of earning one's living. What should it be? Not then could a member of a poor family announce his ambitions (if any), and be allowed to pursue the road to glory forthwith. As usual our Mother came to the rescue. Our world was full of blind-alley jobs but she saw to it that I should follow something with a future, willy-nilly and with no arguments; just as she would have swept us into the kindom of heaven so I was swept into the furniture trade and I found myself apprenticed as a furniture salesman to what was then known as a Complete House Furnisher. It was to be three years of serfdom and the meanest drudgery. There was, however, something else to it, though I was unaware of the silver lining at the time. By a fluke I became a member of one of the most interesting trades in the lists, one in which individuality and artistry could find full scope.

Few today can realize what a furniture shop was like when I entered as a neophyte into the great traditions of Chippendale, Sheraton and Hepplewhite. My starting-place, characteristic of so many others, was the dullest, heaviest, dirtiest and least romantic of shops in general. There was a smell about them that greeted one at the door, and an atmosphere not far short of gloom. They were mortuaries of old dead homes and dust was near to dust, accumulating faster than one could clear it away. Many of these old cabinet-makers and Complete House Furnishers were also undertakers and the relationship was fitting and complementary.

The business I joined was reasonably old-established, having been founded by the principal's father who had drunk himself to death (no wonder). It was hardly surprising that the son was a blue-ribbon man, a dour abstainer. He was also a member of our chapel. The shop had been made out of a large double-fronted house and bore the rather significant number of 99. Strange to say, the head was to reach that number of years. The semi-basement had been covered over and provided an excellent forecourt for the display of goods, while the stabling at the side was converted into more show space. The premises had been a school and at the rear was a large hall with a domed roof of corrugated iron. Upstairs was a series of large rooms all devoted to heavy-weight furniture characteristic of the time, but at the top the windows at the rear gave on to a nursery immediately below. I used to solace myself when not pursuing the every-day scavenging by gazing out to that freedom and dreaming of something other than the dreadful monotony. I was bound to that living death for three weary years, receiving a shilling a week for the first year, three shillings for the next and five shillings for the last. I was destined not to receive those large sums for I was most unfortunate and sometimes had an accident, breaking even the unbreakable. When this happened my money was stopped, even the shilling period, to help pay for the damage done, not, it is true, by the abstainer head but by his brother who I was to find had already been immortalized as Wackford Squeers. Dickens did not exaggerate.

I went first for a month on trial, which was a two-way stretch and I had to provide myself with a black apron. That in itself was an omen, but they did the rest. There was a great deal to know in the furnishing trade, especially if one was to be an all-rounder. It was hinted to my father who took me to be interviewed by the dour, puritan head that I might rise to the astronomical height of five pounds a week in wages and to the wearing of a frock-coat and top-hat. What greater rewards for diligence and industry could one seek? To be a good salesman, to know it all, to be able to give advice even if seldom accepted, to understand the nature, structure and origin of the many complex attributes of a home, to say nothing about the ability to enter into the mind of a woman with an insight equal to a modern psychologist, were to become the pursuit of a lifetime.

As far as my early training was concerned it consisted in cleaning and scavenging and portering heavy loads that all but broke my back and my spirit. I was tutored in the art of brushing upholstered goods, getting into the crevices and corners, and as many of the easy chairs and settees were buttoned there was great scope. Also I was given an oily rag and an evil-looking bottle filled with a viscous fluid known as reviver. This had to be dosed on to a rag and applied to the polished wood frames and surfaces. It was impressed on me that elbow grease was of greater importance than the lotion in restoring a dead article to life. Besides, if one was too liberal, the resultant sticky mass of dust and oil called forth rebukes and even more friction. This horrible concoction used to get into the lines of my hands and it was a job to get them clean.

But that was only part of my job, sweeping and dusting were also included. As the floors were bare the broom was capable of raising a cloud almost as great as the sand-storm I once ex-

perienced travelling from Amman to Jerusalem. This, of course,
had to settle on something and as furniture in those days was
designed as a lodgement and all wardrobes had a cornice and
in most cases a pediment as well, the duster and feather flick
(often hawked round by gipsies) needed never be idle. Besides,
the younger of the two brothers, to make sure I pushed the
broom about, used to tear up the envelopes and bits of paper
and strew them round the rooms. He was a most delightful
creature not fit to possess a dog.

The walls of the shop were lined with pitch-pine match-
boarding and to this were affixed the overmantels which had
many shelves. Then in one part were fixtures containing boxes
of ball fringe. As the shop was lit with gas, the resultant settle-
ment of fine dust on these surfaces, especially the boxes, must
have been a forerunner of the "fall out" of which we often hear.
It had to be tasted to be enjoyed and as far as I remember was
an amalgam of Dr Tibble's Vi-Cocoa and liquorice powder, which
acted on one like an overdose of bromide. To perform this
cleansing at night when the lamps were lit in the dry heat was
almost more than long-suffering youth could endure; and youth
in those days was long suffering and mute withal. The hours
were eight in the morning to eight at night, early closing Saturdays at six. And don't be late or in a hurry to get away. If
brother saw I was looking at the clock he would do his best to
keep me just that bit later.

There were certain unforgiveable offences which were looked
upon almost in the light of sacrilege, such as standing on a
cane-seated chair, or a polished surface, or even an upholstered
seat. Opening a ball of string or twine from the outside, cutting
the string of a parcel instead of carefully undoing the knot,
tearing off paper wrappings instead of undoing and folding them
for another occasion since their uses were infinite.

Not much new furniture crossed our mat except a little art
nouveau in very small doses. It certainly looked a bit incon-
gruous with its heart-shaped apertures, inlays of mother-of-

pearl, enamel and repoussé copper, and elongated tulips, amid the massive weight of Victoriana. However, it was an era of broken hearts amongst women, a disability that has since died out, and of ennui engendered by high art. It certainly aroused my interest as something new in a world that had grown old and static. At that time quaint was a term that had not acquired a sickly sentimental and pejorative meaning. It was an attempt at expressing a period, if it was only "Grosvenor Gallery green-ery-yallery" a phrase applied at the time to designs of the Beardsley art nouveau period, and died in the bud. It has been pointed out that the only large-scale example of art nouveau to be found in London is the meat and poultry hall at Harrods.

Having no money of my own I determined to make myself a wing easy-chair of the variety then illustrated to match these quaint pieces; so I set to work. I made the frame out of ash bedstead sides, rock-like in their heaviness and for the lighter parts I purchased some two-by-two oak. How I sweated as I hewed out this outline which would have held an elephant, let alone my spare person. Then came the ticklish job of upholster-ing it. It is true I got a little professional help, but not a lot and when it was finished and covered in scarlet leather-cloth that rivalled pillar-box red, the upholstered lines were not exactly straight as those shown in the catalogue. I made this chair to be a counterpart to one my grandfather used, which had beauti-ful Georgian lines about it; and it was to be mine when we sat round the fire to read. Alas when it was really ready it was too narrow in the back and I had to sit in it sideways. It became a repository for old newspapers, was never moved since it weighed a ton and perished in the blitz.

Incidentally, whilst I was there the telephone was installed. It was of the primitive type which I notice today is amongst collectors' pieces. I was scared if I was alone and had to answer it. The exchange was at Sydenham and it was a very early number.

Buying, other than at auctions, was an even greater art than selling and was at the foundation of a successful business. Manufacturing in a large way was in the hands of a very few, mostly Polish or Russian Jews who had found a friendly refuge in the congeries of little streets about Shoreditch and Curtain Road, working under the most cramped conditions in their own kitchens and sculleries. Some of these were destined to grow into large factories and to make fortunes. Carcase furniture such as bedroom suites, sideboards, bookcases, cabinets, were to be found here, as were also overmantels and dining tables. Those old seven-piece suites of saddlebag and velvet and leather cloth came from Hoxton, with specialized frame-makers and little else. Chairs, predominantly Windsor but also of the cane-seated variety came from High Wycombe, products of the old chair bodgers. They were often hawked round on countrified wagons from shop to shop. It was many years before that old Buckinghamshire town with its swan badge could produce the carcases for which Shoreditch was famous.

The iron and brass bedsteads came from Birmingham, carpets from Kidderminster, wicker and bamboo furniture from around City Road, oriental carpets, rugs and ornaments from nearer the docks at St Mary Axe. Between Newgate Street and St Paul's in those little streets and squares, were businesses specializing in curtain fabrics, blind hollands and lace, mattress ticks and bed lace (which was the edging for the mattresses), feather-bed ticking and the thousand and one varieties of trimmings, since nothing in those days was left with a plain edge or in what would have been considered an unfinished state. There were fringes for every purpose, not only for curtains at the windows but round the table covers on the mantel drapes and the mats on the floor. The art of the business was to know just where to get this and that and who specialized in this particular thing, whether it was a bit of cabinet ironmongery, bewildering in variety and purpose, or toilet ware for the washstand.

This latter centred about Holborn, and for the benefit of those who have only known a bathroom, consisted of a basin, jug or ewer, chamber pot, brush vase for teeth and soap dish. These items were all duplicated in the case of a double set. As time passed these served not only a necessity but became ornaments, like Swinburne's poetry, "luminous and vivid", shining in all kinds of fantastic shapes and colours on the grim operating tables known as washstands.

The aim and object of all manufacturers in those days centred about endurance. "Would it wear well?" "Yes, it would last a lifetime," not knowing what that promise might mean and forgetting the words of the old Book that moth and rust would corrupt. Yet there were the ever-present deficiencies of sagging beds and seats, chairs that would develop rickets, do what one might. Wicker chairs creaked, bamboo tables wobbled, carpets developed moths, blinds got stuck and the side cords wound round the wretched fittings and all the contingencies of wear and tear manifested themselves. However it was all taken for granted as the price to be paid for comfort and a happy be-laurelled English home.

The art of display had not then come into the picture, it was all hugger-mugger, but then that applied to other kinds of businesses. Windows were crowded in a most utilitarian way and stuff strung about so that every crevice was filled and often the object of search was missed. Yet since furniture and furnishings have an appeal of their own they were as attractive as windows went in those days. I suppose the great change in furniture shops came about when the drapers saw there was money in the merchandise and opened departments where the psychological effects of elevenpence three farthings could have full play on what had been a rather heavy commodity.

Sideboards would be grouped together in one section within the shop, dining tables in another, piled on top of each other; chairs would have a place to themselves, cabinets would line the walls and above them overmantels. Wardrobes would be found somewhere else, dressing tables likewise and washstands coldly apart with their memorial-like tops of white marble with or without holes for the basins. But who today ever sees one of those fantastically shaped suites supposed to represent the period of Louis XVI as conceived by the makers in Bethnal Green? They consisted of a curly-shaped settee with a similarly shaped back in one corner, then straight off to a scroll, before ending in the upright of the arm. They were covered in Genoa velvet and brocade, with two tub easy chairs to match and four chairs with the traditional Louis legs. These adorned the drawing rooms with a tall black cabinet to match, which was really plum-coloured. These consisted of one small cupboard, glass-fronted, the shelves covered in plush, many open shelves and a lot of silvered glass, again shaped, while cast-brass enrichments gave elegance and importance to the handles and even the key holes. If you had enough money you could get one nearly to cover the wall space.

Carpets were of at least five kinds: Brussels, tapestry, Axminster, Wilton and Kidderminster, the last being a flowered drugget made of wool, with an almost everlasting endurance. The hardest wearing was the Brussels, made on a Jacquard loom and woven through to the back. It was equal to public wear and I have seen some at least a century old; but against the lush softness of Axminster it lacked interest. In good-class homes the rooms were close-covered as now and some of the Axminster patterns in floral effects on a black background have never been surpassed. Eau-de-Nil was a colour that became very popular, a shade introduced by the exiled Empress Eugénie. Measuring, making and fitting these carpets, which were of rolls 27 inches wide and 18 inches border, was a great art. Squares were just coming in, eventually to become seamless. In some of the larger establishments the senior salesman would keep a snuffbox to counteract the dust in which they lived.

It should be mentioned in passing that there was one colour only for the dining room and that was red. If you couldn't afford a Turkey carpet you had the next best thing, a turkey-pattern Axminster. This was always considered to be the Englishman's idea of home, with a flock wall-paper to match and copies of Landseer's pictures on the wall and bronze figures of horses on the mantelpiece.

Bedsteads and bedding have been always a problem solved largely in our day by the advent of the divan and spring interior mattress, imported into this country from the States. There was hardly a house without one of the old four poster or half-tester still in use. Some of these have come back again, without the bugs which our grandparents accepted as necessary evils. These had valances round the three sides and behind were stored all kinds of junk including the trunks for next year's holiday. It was the same with the iron beds, many of which were of the tester type that looked extremely nice with their attendant curtains and valances. But all of these were fitted with iron laths interlaced and attached to the iron sides by means of metal buttons. These supported the palliasses and were notable means of collecting dust. Sometime in mid-Victorian years the wire-spring mattresses were evolved, described as sanitary, to replace the palliasses. When the black and brass bedsteads came in the knobs reached pineapple proportions, but some of the all-brass beds were very nice and attractive. Grandmother's bed was not itself without a feather bed, which might be of spiky old chicken's feathers or the soft and really beautiful goose down.

Mattresses were of rather dirty materials; they might be made from old clothes shredded to pieces and sold as rugging or of hair—the latter were warranted to last a lifetime, and did. However, they had a nasty habit of matting up and had to be remade, when the loosening of the dust would have astonished the sleepers could they have seen what was beneath them. The very best of mattresses were made of lambs' wool and soft white hair.

Incidentally the remaking of these mattresses and beds was an awful business for the poor fellow who had to tease the stuff to pieces by means of a machine known as a devil. He had no protection from the dust. Feather beds were treated in a special room known as the feather room, which was thick with cobwebs. He had to beat up the feathers with a stick and the result could be imagined.

In those days of long ago the placid comfort of the English home suffered an upheaval once every year. It was known as spring cleaning. This was the natural outcome of twelve fires roaring up twelve chimneys for the major part of the year and the pea-soup fogs that never failed to descend on us as November and December arrived in the yearly round. The upheaval was complete and life could hardly have been worth living during the period. But that was where the Complete House Furnisher came in. His men were called upon to take up the carpets and beat them, a pretty colossal task considering their size and weight, and then relay them. The curtains were taken down and the cornice poles lifted off their brackets, not omitting the huge pictures that were removed from the special rods that supported them, before picture rails became normal.

And that was where I came in to assist as far as I was able, but it also gave me the opportunity of going into other people's houses and seeing something of how they lived. I remember the bedroom of one local magnate, a solicitor and our town clerk, who evidently wore paper collars. He must have considered himself good for many years, because under his bed were grosses of these in boxes which had to be removed before the floor could be reached and the carpet removed.

Chairs and settees in the drawing-room were shrouded in holland covers and everything was in an uproar. An excellent picture of this stormy period is portrayed in Gwen Raverat's *Period Piece*. One of her uncles who was susceptible to colds was provided with one of these covers all to himself, and sat placidly calm enveloped like a figure in the Ku-Klux-Klan. When it was all over and the fireplaces decked with flowers or paper fans and the lace curtains took the place of the heavy drapes, the next great enemy to moth and rust was the sun, whose beams had to be excluded at all cost; for the dog days were drawing near.

Behind the shops were the workshops, providing a service in maintenance and restoration. Cabinet-makers as such did not produce any furniture—it was like our father's trade of cordwaining, a euphemism; but their workshops were as full of interest as they were full of dust and shavings. The most conspicuous thing was the glue pot bubbling away with its own peculiar smell, while the walls were festooned with old spare parts, members of chairs and tables that might provide just the part required and thus live again. Their time was taken up by renovating and repairing old things and the making of coffins as and when the Reaper reaped. But they were all highly skilled workmen with a fine kit of tools of which they were justly proud.

Polishing was always of interest. The smell of polish was rather nice, and the polish bottles assumed curious shapes caused by the solidified overspill. Some were not above drinking the methylated spirits. It must be remembered that a polished surface was treated with the respect we give to jewellery.

The upholsterers were a many-sided lot working in tapestry, velvets, damasks or moroccos and skins that required the most exact treatment. The foundations for this work called forth great skill in stitching the edges of the seats, giving a clear-cut line and a surface that would not show the indentation of the sitter. This work was usually finished off with leather-covered lead moulding or close brass nails. Sometimes leather work was buttoned, at one time seats as well as backs, which necessitated more exact skill. It was one thing working in soft material, but quite another in leather to get a clean and even crease. They also cut out loose covers and anything else that required special treatment, such as blinds. Some known as Duchess blinds had a lace rising to an apex of design in the insertion. These had to be made specially on machines. The old roller blinds were manipulated by means of an endless cord attached to a flange wheel at the side and fastened to a gadget that held the cord taut, but allowed it to be drawn up and down by pulling at the cord. As the cord loosened, so the attachment could be adjusted, but when the cord broke, oh dear! it was a sore trial. Later a spring roller came into use, patented as usual in America, which was controlled by one short cord in the centre.

But just think of those old sash windows and their dressage. First a blind, then lace curtains both at sides and halfway up the window. At one time there was a vogue for these latter to hang behind a flat brass band fixed across the window pane. Nottingham was the place for lace curtains and women were mighty proud of those fruits of the loom, but the front of the house must match. The wealthier housewives went in for embroidered Swiss curtains and those who liked softness and a graceful hang went in for Madras muslin, which if it originated in India came from Scotland. Behind the lace came heavier fabrics, chintz or dimity in summer and serge, always prefixed by "art" (I have never known why), repp, tapestry, velvet or brocade; all of which required loops and attendant hooks to hold them back in the true professional manner. These curtains hung from what were known as cornice poles, of which the bamboo variety was in greatest evidence. Others of wood, finished white-reeded, walnut, mahogany or oak, were fitted with rings and ends to match, the cheaper varieties being of light brass. Some of the bay poles were made to measure after elaborate measurements had been taken and the angles cut out of the solid, thus providing a smooth run. An early form of curtain railway was an elaborate and expensive track let into a thick brass pole and was controlled by cords. But the fact remained it was still a cornice pole and was fixed and looked as such.

Furniture vans in those days were huge tilted affairs and in the case of my first employer the horses were hired, but one outside man accompanied the driver. When those large easy chairs and settees were collected for renovation, the first thing the men did when the goods were safely out of sight was to go down the seats between the arms and the back and sides with their hands. It was often a rewarding search with a bit of silver or gold, but care had to be taken lest the only recompense should be the business end of a knitting needle or the point of a pair of scissors. Sometimes the reward lay with the ripper-open of the article, the prize being too deep for exploring fingers.

Household removals were an essential service. There were houses in plenty and a large number empty, so removals from one desirable residence to another was a daily occurrence. For this service sundry large vans known as pantechnicons with low wheels were maintained, drawn by two or more horses. One or more of these would arrive at an early hour, pull in at the kerbside or in the drive, the tailboard would be used as a ramp, and loaded up. These vans always smelt fragrantly of Russian mats, which were soft and made from a rush or reed. The men wore a green baize apron which was as much a mark of their calling as the grocer's or the butcher's. If the removal was to a long distance the van would go by rail on a bogey or the contents unloaded into a railway truck and arrangements made to unload it the other end. Later on lift vans were instituted, known as a tunnel van because it would pass through a tunnel.

When I was with my second employer he was one of the first to possess a Foden steam wagon, which enabled him to do long-distance work from door to door. This cavalcade of van and wagon was a novel sight and was the beginning of road transport away from the railways. It was a nine days' wonder, dropping hot cinders and sparks as it trundled along, putting the horses to fright. The contents of a house then was always reckoned by weight and a clever estimator could assess it to within a few pounds. Now it is a matter of cubic capacity.

Days moved slowly, so slowly, when hours were of more than sixty fleeting minutes and my apprenticeship came to an end. I was no longer wanted even at five shillings a week. Labour was cheap and a secure job none too easy to find, but I got fixed up with a rival firm, more enterprising it is true but with too many

A corner of old Felixstowe

Opening an exhibition at Walberswick, Suffolk

irons in the fire to have a secure future. Neither was the pay anything to brag about and I was to run into the biggest lot of self-helps I have ever met. It was probably the result of poor wages, but it was a disease that affected both high and low.

The head was a public-spirited man who never seemed to have a moment to spare. The business was at a corner overlooking the railway station and when he wanted to catch a train he would wait until the distant signal fell, then run and arrive as the train drew into the station. Much of his energy was spent in beating the air. However, rather like the doctors he sported a very nice little pony and trap with a groom to carry out his appointments. Later he ran a de Dion Bouton car. I stayed there too long, but my turn was to come, though not yet.

My next job, which was an attempt at striking out, was at a nearby suburb well-known to Dr Johnson where his great friend Mrs Thrale lived. It was then throwing up a mushroom growth of houses and I found myself with two brothers far more enterprising than the first two, who were associated in the building of some of those villas. Their name was soon to loom large in the building-contracting world, but at that time they were running a small furnishing shop that was again a converted private house, in a road leading to the lavender fields of Mitcham and to Brock's fireworks factory. But oh those hours, they were the worst ever, eight-thirty in the morning to nine at night, ten on Fridays and eleven on Saturdays. And once more the rule was: don't be in a hurry to get away. I stuck it as long as I could, was interested in the scope of the job, was earning more money and liked the brothers who appeared to like me. But I couldn't stand those hours, so I gave notice and left.

It is a curious reflection on the shopping public, then as now, that however long the hours they are never long enough. My last customer at that shop was a young couple about to furnish. I had had them before but they came to place their order at about ten-thirty on the Saturday night and I was kept there nearly until Sunday morning. But those were the days when the butchers sold off their meat by auction on that night to a surging public.

Whilst here I had to have my meals at a cookshop. There I met a promising young butcher who let me into one of the secrets of that trade. One item of his training was the ability by sleight of hand to "dutch" the scales and so make up the profits.

Needless to say I didn't jump out of that job until I had got another and this time it was to the desideratum of all shop assistants, Oxford Street itself. What a wonderful chance, thought I. Now were the tail-coat days really coming to pass, for such was the essential of anyone employed in the West End. It was necessary to catch an early train to Victoria and I remember being intrigued by the eighteenth-century shop fronts of Bond Street, as I made my way to that basement prison where I staffed a department alone. But what a change in hours almost heavenly: nine to six and one o'clock on Saturdays. What could be better? Alas, I was not destined to remain there long, no-one would come and relieve me for meals, I saw few customers, so I asked for a rise and got the sack, a cynical letter and a moment's notice. I thought the world had come to an end. But it hadn't, at least not for me, although it had for many.

One morning on my way to catch my train I noticed the placards announcing an assassination. It was the tragic end of the Archduke and Duchess of Austria-Hungary, the spark that was to set the world alight. I passed on and thought no more about it, little recking it was to change all our lives. Neither had I the faintest idea where such a place as Sarajevo was. I little dreamed that one day I should find myself there, standing on the very spot where the shot was fired and feeling stunned that there I should see the assassin idealized as a national hero. However it was on a par with being taken round the infamous camp at Buchenwald by a German woman guide.

I left Oxford Street to the tramping feet of enthusiastic volunteers. In that store one of the pattern-room staff was a young German, but he disappeared as suddenly as the skies darkened. I often wonder what became of him. After all he was one of many so employed, ostensibly to learn the language.

In my dejection one morning scanning the columns of Situations Vacant, I came across an advertisement for a soft-furnishing assistant in a nearby market town. I hurried off and before I knew where I was I found myself engaged, rather alarmingly as I thought as I knew so little about that side of the business. I voiced my fears and my ignorance but was told I would do. It appeared that some of their staff had left them for the war and they were anxious to fill their places. It was a high-class family business and tail-coats were again *de rigueur*. In fact I managed to wear out whilst here my brother's frockcoat which he had ordered for his wedding that never came off. After a long wait and a poor start my chance had come and I seized it with all my might. I had become the chief support of my father and mother, neither was I at all brave, and those were the reasons why I had not joined up although I was soon to do so. Under ordinary circumstances that type of house would never have looked at me. Also I began to earn money, because we were paid a monthy salary and they had a system of premiums on almost everything sold, which latter were paid weekly and amounted to more than the salary.

I was now required to live in, which was an entirely new experience. But what an uplift in my circumstances that was to prove and how grateful I was for the change. One thing that loomed large was a hot bath once a week, something which I had never enjoyed before. Our bedrooms, which were in the old part of the building, had bare floors, it is true, but they were scrubbed white and one could have eaten one's meals off them. We slept two in a room in spotlessly clean beds and the food was excellent, cooked by the genial old sister who looked after the male side, while her more prim elder half looked after the girls; moreover we could have as much food as we could eat. I shall never forget that lift-up in my life which took me outside the limitations of my old home, of which I was unaware until the wider door opened. As we lay in bed we could hear the horse-drawn market carts making their way from the Kent fields to Covent Garden, the drivers probably fast asleep.

The atmosphere of business in those now far-away days was peculiar. The great slogan bandied about was "Business as Usual". This was voiced from a desperate fear that commercial prosperity might come to an end, but it came to mean that business was most unusual and of a volume never experienced before. That high-class family business which had sprung out of one shop must have made fortunes during those grim and awful years because taxation was nothing comparable with that of today. Whereas blankets, flannel, towels and the like had been sold over the counter in small quantities for personal requirements now they were going out in wholesale consignments to furnish the local hospitals that were being opened up all round in those beautiful outlying districts and homes. In my early days there it was a nightly event to go to the local station and watch the arrival of the sick and wounded from the battle fronts of France and Flanders.

One little peculiarity of those days and the department in which I served was the sale of small silk flags of the Allies for use on bicycles and cars. They became an expression of patriotism now forgotten, but which can be found in the volumes of *Punch* for the period. I forget how many went to the complement but I remember the Japanese Sun was one.

Immediately behind the premises was the old parish church (which was to be gutted by fire in the next great war). It was set in a garden of roses. I have spent many a blissful hour sitting on the grass, back to a gravestone reading during the brief midday break. Under the mat by the west door lay Dr Johnson's Tetty, whilst in one of our bedrooms H. G. Wells was born. His father had kept a small china shop which had been absorbed by our prosperous draper head.

The clientèle was mostly ladies who would arrive in their

carriages and cars soon after ten o'clock in the morning by which time our coats had to be on. They all seemed to run accounts and but little money passed through our hands save at sale times. Moreover, as assistants we were under a fairly strict discipline, for we were not allowed to smoke during business hours, not even in the dinner time, the argument being that our breath might prove offensive to a lady whilst being served, surely a hangover from Victorianism. Neither were we allowed into our bedrooms once we had left them in the morning. On engagement we were presented with a book of rules which I wish I still possessed as a museum piece of other days and ways. They used to recruit young girls as apprentices straight from school. Some would be placed in one or other of the cash desks and be expected to keep the money correctly. If it was short they lost the bonus half-crown awarded for the purpose weekly.

Our monthly salary was paid to us by the head himself in his small mahogany-lined private office. The immediate recipient before the next in line would come into the department with the discreet information that one's presence was required. Whereupon, if disengaged, one would make one's way into the sanctum and be paid out in coin, first having signed one's name in a large ledger over a twopenny stamp, the twopence having been deducted from one's pay. It was quite a pleasant little ritual when one came face to face with the head of a personal business.

Another feature of that very nice house was the sprinkling of apprentices who came for a two-year training. They were nearly all sons of business men and were to return to their own family businesses. Part of the training was sweeping out the various departments at the close of the day and dusting and removing the wrappers in the morning. For the first six months they were given a season ticket on the railway and became what was known as city matchers—that is they had to try and locate the source of materials for special orders and bring back small requirements from the wholesale houses. It was considered an excellent insight into, and groundwork of the trade.

The head, a wealthy quiet man, lived an unostentatious life on a few hundred a year, in a small house in a road not far from his business. He  had no children but was content to be served by his cousin and sundry nephews. He possessed no motor car or carriage and was not on the telephone. Such amenities were in no way essential to his way of life. His wife, as unassuming and kind as he, would sometimes come into the department and make a purchase, not omitting to make enquiries about one's own family life. I was never to meet the like again; and it was from this setting that after a few months I passed into the army.

# II

# Army Days

By those white cliffs I never more must see,
By that dear language which I spake like thee,
Forget all feuds, and shed one English tear
O'er English dust. A broken heart lies here.

MACAULAY

I took the oath and the shilling at Bromley, Kent, was given a railway warrant and sent home with the kindly advice of an old peace-time sergeant-major ringing in my ears. This amounted to the fact that I should take a good razor with me as the army issue was not of much use, and a cake if my mother had one. So the next day or the day after I went by train from East Croydon to Eastbourne, my mother seeing me off. On arrival I must have been met and escorted to Whitbread Hole, Beachy Head. It was to prove one of the most wonderful experiences of my life, especially the first night's sleep on the ground to one who had never slept outside a bed. That camping ground seemed so vast, but when I have gone there since it seems so small.

The first thing was to be given a number on a little piece of card and eventually a new uniform with an ill-fitting overcoat. That sea air engendered a raging appetite which those flat army loaves, butter and jam could certainly assuage, but it was difficult to eat an army stew without knife, fork and spoon. However all in good time one got into the routine and even enjoyed living under a Sussex heaven. Life had a new interest, watching other recruits coming in; and one's loneliness was partially dispelled by the arrival of the mail. How joyful it was to hear one's name called, perhaps more than once and to get a letter—although I was somewhat nonplussed to receive a parcel from home that contained a feather pillow, but it served a turn. We were not allowed out of the camp without a little cane which we had to buy out of our shilling a day; this was to prevent us putting our hands in our pockets when walking. This camp life came to a sudden end because it was autumn, the rain fell and all but flooded us out and we were installed in billets in the town.

All this is indelibly stamped on the memory. To go down that old chalky winding path on Beachy Head today revives too vividly the carefree laughter of those quondam soldiers, the majority of whom are now no more. In the tangled mass behind the iron rails that line the cliff's edge is the fragrant sweet briar, which seems to be a fitting memorial to those young men who, after all, did not grow old with the years. The path is silent now except for the favoured young whose playing fields were once our camp. That well-appointed training ground is a tale that is told.

But it was not from Eastbourne that we went to France because as we neared Christmas we were whisked off to Twezeldown Camp, otherwise known as Haigh Hutments. By this time we had formed friendships and watched the peculiar trait in the human character of like meeting like. Almost the last parade in that old Eastbourne camp and by accident of position when falling in, we had been formed into three field ambulances the 132, 133, and 134. I was for the 133, of the 39th Division.

We entrained early in March 1916 from Southampton for Le Havre, which port was reached in a blinding snow storm; and remember, it was an old France that greeted us. I recall the old shops as we climbed out of the town for our camp which was deep in virgin snow; but oh, what a warm and comfortable night it was, although our ablutions were rather draughty in the morning but we were soon at the railhead to be herded into trucks labelled 'Hommes 40, Chevaux 8'.

What a journey that was, rumbling on and on, now towards

Paris, now away. Through the flat agricultural country of Normandy, past hamlets clustering round their church, though they were so unlike an English village; through this town and that. Evening came and still we journeyed on amid snow and shadows, watching, until eyes could trace no longer the slender trees with tufted tops or the crude mysterious outlines of many buildings set against a wintry sky. The old engine whistled shrilly and still we rumbled on.

The night was passed in fitful sleeping for there was hardly room to stretch one's legs, whilst the intense cold came in through the cracks of the floor and door. Before dawn we found ourselves at St Omer, then the headquarters of the British Army and where Lord Roberts had died. But we rumbled on to the Hazebrouck area and detrained at Steenbecq. We now made our first acquaintance with those straight tree-lined roads evidently built by military engineers with that one obsession at the back of a continental mind-war. Our way lay through the Forêt de Nieppe on through Merville to Estaires.

That first march was to be crammed with interest. The quaint little homesteads of northern France with the cross worked into the tiles of the gabled roofs. The large wheels attached to the sides of their little farmsteads worked by a dog treadmill fashion for churning purposes within the kitchen. Dogs were generally used for drawing rather large carts, filled too often by the bulky owners. Then there was the unequal yoking of oxen and ponies in the creaking agricultural vehicles.

We now received that essential portion of our complement, the mechanical transport, although we had also the old horsed ambulances. They were Fords and Sunbeams. The work which the former accomplished made possible by their high clearance was amazing, to say nothing of the intrepidity of the drivers. On the occasions of attacks the Fords were used almost into the front line.

Our arrival in France was at a time when the fighting was quiet. The area to which we were drafted had become historical as a result of much bloodshed. Names of little places had grown to momentous significance by reason of the heroism of regiments and individuals. Two battles fought around the shambles that was Ypres, Lens, and Neuve Chapelle, had provided a bloody sacrifice of English youth. Hill 60 had been won at the cost of hard fighting. Festubert and Givenchy and Loos had added lustre to British arms, given opportunity for deeds of valour recognized by numerous V.C.s made many a home sad with the memory of those who would never return. But the Somme was not yet nor the bloody fighting of St Julien and Passchendaele.

An observer as he entered the war zone for the first time could not but be impressed by the immense amount of organization that had taken place. The struggle had settled down to what looked like a static war, a sort of new way of life. We entered a field mapped out and prepared, built on the labour and sacrifice of others. The serried rows of guardsmen's crosses in Poperinghe cemetery told how England stood before the greatest onslaught of her time in the Salient which we were later to know so well.

Our first work was of a light and initial nature, for we had still much to learn, and consisted chiefly of running divisional rest stations and taking care of the sick rather than wounded. We were allocated the college at Estaires, with billets for some lower down the Doulieu Road in outhouses. Some eighty rats were killed at this latter and laid out for the C.O.'s inspection. One man placed his mess tin on a beam overhead and during the night an exploring rat knocked it down, scoring a direct hit on the unfortunate owner's head.

Estaires was a somewhat dirty little town, with mud-bespattered walls complete with church, square, *hôtel de ville* and, not least, the Café du Commerce. It was very characteristic of northern France as we were to discover, yet it held the amenities of a few shops where blacking, soap and tooth powder vied with lace, post cards and eatables in one common display. Here we were introduced to the everlasting standby of hungry Tommies

—eggs, chips and coffee. Cognac and the dear delights of over-crowded *estaminets* with the nightly game of House, provided variations for those who indulged in stronger things. Here too we met with admiration old timers, men who had been out since 1914 and therefore knew all there was to know about the eternal war. Some were tunnellers with their thigh boots, on mysterious missions in the line, who spent their hours here between their labours in the trenches.

We were soon on the move, this time crossing little bridges over the Lys into La Gorgue which was notorious for cock fights usually held on a Sunday. Our destination was Calonne-sur-la-Lys. This march provided great interest, past whitewashed walls of quiet homesteads with lichened roofs, over canals with their quaint drawbridges and by the steam tramways that plied along the roadside about these parts, drawn by dirty primitive smoky engines with a shrill whistle.

Whilst in this district the spring rains, that seemed to continue for the rest of the year for that matter, were much in evidence. Rain was an almost continuous development so that the Lys was full to overflowing, like its tributaries. We also discovered the amenities of farmhouse kitchens, sat round their curious little stoves with one red spot of fire, drank milk and ate innumerable eggs and generally made ourselves agreeable to Madame and Mademoiselle. Now was the thrifty husband-man busy in the fields but who can ever forget the sabbaths when they unlocked the cesspits and spread the contents on the fields. It polluted the air for miles around and was more than equal to any gas attack.

Trips to Merville relieved the monotony—the town had a fascinating collection of gabled roofs, shops and canteens. The church was worthy of mention, a modern structure replacing several earlier foundations as its series of windows told. These represented the sad and chequered history of pillage, fire and destruction of the earlier Merville and its church. Alas, 1918 was to see again the town sacked and destroyed, its church razed to the ground when the Germans made their advance and both Estaires and Merville fell into their hands.

Having now become acclimatized to the surroundings and the work, our division proceeded to take its place in the line. We relieved the 38th Division in the Givenchy and Festubert section of the XIth Corps front. The 133 Field Ambulance now moved to the White House at Essars with its pleasant little gardens. The Main Dressing Station was responsible for Lone Farm, Givenchy as an advanced Dressing Station with Aid Posts at South More, Lambeth Road, Queens Road and Sidbury. Lone Farm was the shell of an old building situated between Westminster Bridge on the La Bassée Canal and Windy Corner, which was the entrance to the trenches through a derelict baker's shop. At this period of the year these communication trenches were particularly beautiful, alive with spring flowers behind the wire netting that protected the crumbling sides. Windy Corner was so named because it was not exactly a health resort.

Béthune with all its waterways was the mecca of this district. Who can forget its pleasant tree-lined roads, the shops that enclosed the cobbled square and the old roofs that gave an air of friendly medievalness to the old town. The tower with its belfry high over the quaint old shops that stood in the middle of the square and the magnificent old church. The war had troubled this pleasant place but little.

Béthune provided a thousand joys to relieve the life of a soldier. All tastes and ranks were provided for, the officers made use of the Au Paon d'Or, the Café du Globe or the Officers' Club, the other ranks enjoyed various restaurants according to their means. There were many attractive shops, some made more so by the assistants, notably a boot shop in a side street where two engaging damsels conducted a flourishing trade. Rumour at the time credited them with being spies. Sad to relate, old Béthune of Hugo's days passed entirely away.

As far as I was concerned I was doing duty at Lone Farm when I was told to return to headquarters at Béthune because

I was to go to Divisional Headquarters as the A.D.M.S. wanted an orderly. I did not seek this move and almost resented it but it probably saved my life. I was certainly to see things from a different angle. I often wonder why I was chosen as, pursuing a similar course in the Army to that of my days at school. I was no fine specimen of a soldier. I was to stay on at the H.Q. until the Division was smashed. I must add this, my admiration of the various staff officers whom I saw at work mounted very high. They seemed to work night and day. One of these was Lord Dunmore V.C. and another a Captain Paget who was also a water diviner. Also I can never forget marching off from Béthune one sunny Sunday morning, complete with a new pair of trousers and boots, which I badly needed, to Locon.

Incidentally, leaving Lone Farm as I did, I escaped a very sad sight of which army orders in those days were capable, viz. the execution of an older and younger soldier for alleged coward-ice. A truly horrible business. It was on a par with Field Punishment No. 1, a degrading sight of an English soldier tied to a cart wheel in full view of the local population. Later on I was to know of the great efforts made by our A.D.M.S., an old regular from the South African War days, to save the life of a poor youth, all to no purpose, shot at dawn one bright morning according to the rule book. Our own men placed crosses over the newly dug graves.

The division now was fully employed, often in fruitless but costly night raids about Festubert in this war of attrition. However, August saw us withdrawn from this area and placed in army reserve; we were destined for the Somme, which we were to reach via St Pol, then a delightful spot indeed.

The Somme was a pleasant contrast to the Béthune area, The rolling downs, reminiscent of Sussex, and the countryside were at the height of their summer glory. Around St Pol the villages were ideally pretty with flower-bedecked gardens. The water was drawn from deeper wells, but as we drew near the line con-ditions were more squalid and the plague of flies had to be seen to be believed. We were now close to Albert with its ruined streets, shattered houses, dismantled shops and derelict business premises. The chief feature was the comparatively modern basilica with its battered walls and the huge Madonna and Child leaning at right angles to the tower. Rumour had it that when it fell the war would end. Most soldiers were hoping it would without further delay.

The fighting here was intense and the casualties heavy. One little incident is worth recording, told by a stretcher-bearer bringing down cases amid shell fire. A shell had dropped near them and one man had his leg blown off. The bearer asked if he was all right but the answer came: "Do to me what my wife would do if she was here." The bearer said, "I bent over him and kissed him as he passed away in my arms."

Conditions at this time were appalling. The food was of the poorest, with the result that the men's health suffered severely. Diarrhoea accompanied with the passing of blood was prevalent. Paisley Dump which was beside a narrow bridge over the Ancre and consisted of a low confined dug-out formerly used by the French, running under a bank was packed with men so closely they could hardly lie down to sleep. It was practically full of vermin, the lice even dropping from the ceiling, rats too were in abundance, many of whom were so fat they were an easy prey. It was also said that the trenches in the Thiepval area were knee-deep in gluey mud.

The division was now relieved on the whole front by the 19th Division in mid-November passing out from the IInd Corps to the VIIIth Corps area. It is understood that the senior N.C.O. distinguished himself on this occasion by reporting to the C.O.: "The men are all in the train, sir, ready for marching off."

The Somme left many memories, individual and intimate, but to me there remains the imperishable picture of a line of traffic moving over adjoining hills, silhouetted against the amber light of the setting sun. Guns, limbers, horses, men in a human frieze of the utmost beauty, worthy of a war memorial.

The summer having proved a somewhat muddy and hectic campaign we were pleased to arrive at the quaint and quiet villages of the Esquelbec area. At one village for instance there was a perfect example of almost medievalism with its cobbled streets, ancient church with carillon and a fine specimen of a moated castle. Here indeed was Flanders, the country of the Van Eycks. We were now in the Second Army under General Sir Herbert Plumer. The division now made its acquaintance with the most famous of all war cities, Ypres and was to be there longer than any other of the British Army. In the city itself were two of the finest dressing stations on the Western Front, one at the prison the other at the asylum.

A visit to Ypres left an impression of awe: ruined limbers and dead horses lay in the square. Men moved as quickly as possible from wall to wall, while ever and anon shrieking shells made greater gaps in ruined walls, ploughed larger holes in pitted roads, disinterred the broken dead or spent themselves upon the scarred ramparts. One grave on that old fortification was that of Prince Maurice Battenberg, son of Princess Beatrice, a very early casualty. The Germans well knew that the whole of this immense Salient had to be served through this city, which was the one and only key.

If Ypres was the key of the Salient, Poperinghe was the key of Ypres, for the one main road that passed through the centre was the only way by which troops and transport could pass along to their destination. Strategically, of course, it was enormously important, for here was the railhead. The town hall abutted on to the main road on the outskirts nearer Ypres and here was displayed the famous sign "Wind Safe" or "Wind Dangerous". Between Pop and Ypres was that dangerous stretch of tree-lined, cobbled road that led straight through Vlamertinghe, along which all troops and transport must pass. The throbbing, clattering stream that ever passed and turned this once quiet rural district into one of the busiest thoroughfares night and day. At our time it seemed to be the main artery of the war. It might also be mentioned that in the town itself was born one of the most remarkable institutions of the war, known as Talbot House under the aegis of the Rev. P. B. Clayton, otherwise Tubby Clayton to most soldiers. The town was continually under shell fire from long-range guns.

We were to be in and out of the line, transferred from the VIIIth to the XVIIIth Corps and in time for the Third Battle of Ypres, after which a new feature developed in aircraft activity by the enemy. This was carried out between lights each day as the moon and the weather permitted. The bombers came over in relays fairly shovelling out the bombs. Then came that most astonishing *débâcle* to be known as Passchendaele. How we waited and watched the weather deteriorate until the ground was almost impossible; even I, a poor ignorant private was aghast at such folly with men's lives, ordered by those who never soiled their boots.

1918 was to be to us as to all units a most memorable year, perhaps more so to ourselves. It was therefore with great excitement we received news towards the end of January that we were to leave the Salient, but it was a case once again of the frying pan and the fire, because we found ourselves back on the Somme to be part of the Fifth Army in time for the Great Retreat. What an occasion, because we knew the day and almost the very minute when the attack was to take place. Preparations had been made, it is true, but some of the defensive lines merely consisted of coloured ribbons. How swiftly our armies fell back and how swiftly the roads became blocked, but I never saw or heard a word of complaint or despair, everyone was so glad to be out of a static war. During this retreat we lost our divisional general, Major-General Feetham who was killed by a shell splinter in the neck. He was a fine and fearless soldier beloved by all.

The retreat was perhaps the most remarkable experience we were called upon to pass through. It commenced in the barren and stricken country about Gouzecourt and ended, so far as we were concerned in the pleasantly wooded country west of Amiens. The war, however, was not over, although our division was sadly broken and became known as the 39th Division Composite Brigade and we rushed back to the Salient where the line had given way by the Portuguese, necessitating the withdrawal of the whole Second Army front. But we were accorded some rest in the lovely summer country around Calais, which centuries before had been the scene of that scintillating pageant of the Field of the Cloth of Gold. After this we were destined to be tutors to the medical units of the American Expeditionary Force which had now entered the war.

11th November 1918 saw us in the Somme area again, suffering in a small degree from the influenza epidemic that was to kill off so many of those who had escaped from the terror of war. As far as I was concerned I was transferred to another unit, came home on leave, got demobbed and did not return, feeling as a result very lonely. It was a wonderful spirit that pervaded that Great War even to the end, symbolized by the word "Chum". And I was to make friendships that have lasted a lifetime.

> Now a' is done that man can do,
> And a' is done in vain.
> ROBERT BURNS

# The Road Back

---

Because the road is rough and long,
Shall we despise the skylark's song?
ANNE BRONTË

Demobilization saw me back in the job I had left. The buyer I had been under had enlisted after me and been killed almost as soon as he had reached France leaving behind a little family. He had had a presentiment that that would happen. I found it difficult to settle down. Then my father died, poor old man, an awful death by empyema, conscious to the end; this was to be the first break in our home life.

I was always a great reader, trying to supplement the very limited education I had received. I attended some extension lectures on the Italian Renaissance which had a great influence on me and read Roscoe's *Life of the Medici*. Greatly daring by some means or other, I mapped out a route and set off for Florence during my fortnight's holiday. This was, long before the advent of the package tour.

I went via Newhaven to Dieppe and thence to Paris, spent a day or two sightseeing which included the Louvre, Notre Dame, Napoleon's Tomb, the Arc de Triomphe, the Tuileries and the Eiffel Tower; by a moment's hesitation I missed Versailles, which I have always regretted. From Paris I took the train to Milan and shall never forget the stop at the frontier station of Modane or the coffee and fresh rolls and butter that were available while the train waited for checking before going through the Simplon Tunnel. On arrival at Milan I must have found somewhere to sleep but as soon as that was settled I was out looking for the cathedral. As I turned a corner this mountain of stone loomed up before me, an unforgettable sight. But still more wonderful was the roof and the forest of statuary. There I met a R.C. priest who was on his way to Rome and wanted me to go with him, but I was for Venice, so he said he would wait for me in Florence.

The next day I set off for Venice. Although I cut my stay short I saw much. I found lodging on the Schiavone and was soon inside St Mark's, noting the four bronze horses on the west front and the notice against spitting inside. There was also the Doges' Palace and the Campanile which had not yet fallen, and I managed a trip in a gondola, which inevitably led to a glass warehouse.

I found walking about Venice rather pleasing, a city without traffic and with the Rialto Bridge in the midst like the Bridge of Sighs, but there was a decided smell about the canals. However, I left with a mental picture of the sun on the dome of Santa Maria della Salute, made famous by Turner and the memories of Canalettos and Tintorettos. And so to Florence.

I duly met the priest, who was useful in conducting me to the English Protestant cemetery, but how blazing hot it was and everywhere covered with the dreadful white dust. I was indebted to my quondam friend for the visit to this place which I should never have found by myself. First came the ornate sarcophagus of Elizabeth Browning by Lord Leighton and nearby the grave of Arthur Hugh Clough, friend of Florence Nightingale, sometime Fellow of Oriel College, Oxford. His verse will always be held in great esteem because Winston Churchill quoted it at a time when England was in her greatest straits. Fanny Waugh Hunt, wife of Holman Hunt the Pre-Raphaelite is another; she died in the first year of her marriage, 1866. Mrs Trollope, mother of Anthony lies there. The simplest grave of all is of that strange figure, said to have been a perfect example

of King Lear in real life, Walter Savage Landor. It is surrounded
with bay leaves and bears Swinburne's epitaph:

And thou, his Florence, to thy trust receive and keep
　　Keep safe his dedicated dust
　　　　His sacred sleep.
　　So shall thy lovers come from afar
　　　　Mix with thy name
　　As morning star with evening star
　　　　His faultless name.

My friend then left for Rome and I was to wander into the
vast Duomo, see Ghiberti's bronze doors to the Baptistry,
Giotto's tower and that marvellous survival, the Ponte Vecchio.
It was cool and refreshing along the banks of the Arno, but I
remember seeing placards by the waterside bearing a name that
was to have great significance to us all within a few years, that
of Mussolini. I saw some of the great pictures in the galleries
and pursued Perugino's "Crucifixion" until I found it. I also
saw the wonderful Medici Chapel and the Westminster Abbey
of Italy, Santa Croce. I came home through Genoa and just
had enough strength to visit the famous Campo Santo, although what with the heat and the water I drank I must have
caught a slight attack of typhoid or enteritis because the sanitation was awful.

A year or two went by before I managed to get back to
France and the Ypres battle area. They were busy concentrating
the bodies of the fallen into the now famous War Cemeteries.
I queried the word "body" with one man, who assured me such
was the case because the mud had acted as a preservative. I
managed to visit Béthune and almost wished I hadn't, because
it was entirely rebuilt, a raw township with all its old romance
gone.

I now began to get a bit restive in my job, so with great re-
luctance I took a post in Canterbury with an old-established
business. It did not work and I was out in three months, feeling very sorry and a failure. Soon afterwards I took a job in

Gosport as a stop gap, and when the spring came went home and got another at Kingston-upon-Thames. It was a curious experience that was to change my whole life. The head was one of those business giants who, although somewhat austere, was a very kind man at heart, especially attached to children. He did his good deeds surreptitiously. Yet, one must remember those were the days of a moment's notice.

Whilst there my mother died of malnutrition due to religious mania. She had literally starved herself to death. I was sitting with her by the fire one day, she in her dressing gown, when she happened to stretch out her leg which was only a bone. I was shocked. Both parents are buried in the *un*consecrated portion of the cemetery.

Now came my next venture abroad. I consulted the son of the head, asked for a month off and went to Norway on a cruise, leaving Newcastle one hot summer's day and arriving at Bergen after a squally voyage. I did not appreciate this visit to such a lonely land where it seemed to rain every other day. Neither did I welcome the mountain roads in their open motor charabancs, which seemed so dangerous. I remember how the people on one side of the dining saloon suddenly got up and cheered because they had seen a cow; and how vivid was the grass. But I did not miss the Hanseatic Museum.

So with the strange purpose that governs life I went back to Kingston where I met my wife who was of an old East Molesey family named Kemp. The Kemps have been traced back to 1794 in that place, one member being a night watchman and another probably a seamstress at Hampton Court Palace. Gwynne Sylvia Estelle was in the telephone exchange of that business house, her voice was soft and pleasant and we used to go for long walks into Surrey at the week-ends. After one such tramp we pulled up at an hotel in Virginia Water to a most delightful tea. I suggested it would be an ideal place for a honeymoon and she thought so too. Believe it or not, I did not know the first thing about getting married, sought the advice of a vicar who thought I was mad, but as I did not want the banns called I was directed to get a licence. The registrar remarked about the spelling of my name, should it not have an 'e' in it? I told him he was probably correct as my people came from the eastern side of England and may well have originated in Scandinavia. So we were married, she sixteen years my junior, in Kingston Parish Church, waiting for it to strike eight, with two witnesses on Christmas Eve 1929. It has been a lasting and happy bond.

On looking back it was rather a rash step, we parted that morning, she to her job and me to mine. We did not meet again until the next morning when we journeyed to Virginia Water for our projected honeymoon of three days. We had no home or the prospect of one, but when the news got about at my old home a relative soon found us a flat in Belvedere Road, Upper Norwood. I furnished it *à la mode* with the latest ideas and we started housekeeping. It was a happy carefree existence while it lasted because I was firmly convinced that employment at that expanding store was no place for a married man so I got a job with an old-established high-class firm at Southsea. That also proved a chimera and once again I found myself out of work. However, providence intervened and I was back in south London.

Our first child was born on Good Friday, 1931 and I can never forget the thrill with which I gazed at the little creature with dark hair, who appeared even at first sight to smile at me. I seemed to walk on air. Surely there are moments in one's life that are tinged with gold. There certainly have been in mine, which warrant illuminating like the initial letters in a Book of Hours.

I was now getting into my job, in charge at last, but we were none too comfortably housed in a so-called flat with no amenities. It therefore behoved me to get a place of my own. As I write this in 1975 it seems an incredible tale that I could go and buy a new semi-detached with room for a garage for five pounds deposit, but such was the case. As I look back I think it was the foundation of my small fortune because I got an overdraft from a bank with the understanding of monthly repayments. How zealously I scraped the money together and watched the debt go down until it was cleared.

I had been always keen on writing and can recall the joy with which I received my first half-crown from, I think, a periodical called the *Newspaper World*. If one got a paragraph accepted one received a postal order or stamps in a little buff-coloured envelope on a Friday night or Saturday morning. Eventually I began to write for a trade journal, but now I got the chance of writing my first book; it happened this way. The Field Ambulance to which I had belonged began reunion dinners in London. An officer suggested it would be nice to have a permanent record made. The idea was enthusiastically welcomed, but as there were no volunteers I rashly offered to do it; naturally I got the job. The result was another of those golden moments when the reality appeared. True it was very amateurish but it was a dream fulfilled. Anticipating things somewhat, an even greater thrill was when I got an article accepted by *Country Life*, that gentlemanly and splendid magazine; this led to a series in that journal which in turn led to another book.

Within a year or so a son was born to us, then came the gap of a few years when another boy appeared who was to complete our family. As I passed to work I used to notice a rather interesting-looking house bearing the name of Beauchamp Cottage just within the boundary of Lambeth, then came the day when it was up for sale and I bought it.

What a wonderful old place it was, really one or two farm cottages made into one long house, with a long garden in front ending in a fine oak tree and a longer garden at the rear with many fruit trees, including two of the most luscious pear-trees I have ever known. The fruit melted in the mouth. There was also a Marie Louise, the fruit of which I sold to Fortnum and Mason of Piccadilly. Near the house was one of the prettiest trees, a little quince; the fruit when it ripened looked like

Chinese lanterns amid the dark green leaves. Another tree was a hornbeam that used to bleed.

A previous owner had erected a porch over the front door which she had carved, bearing the words *Vale* and *Salve* on the two posts and a Latin inscription on the little gable roof, a play on 'Beauchamp', meaning "The lot is fallen to me in a fair ground".

It was indeed an extraordinary house, particularly the plumbing in the roof. If we left the place for a week we got an air-lock in the bathroom which I tried to correct with the nozzle of an early vacuum cleaner. It was a wonder I didn't get electrocuted. We got burst pipes in the summer if it was a bit hot and of course at the slightest appearance of frost. An old man, full of character, used to come and mend these. In his time he had mended the metal angel at the convent which used to scare me as a child passing it with my mother on our way to West Norwood cemetery. Incidentally that old resting-place of south London magnates and others received more than one bomb, one of which blew off the front of Spurgeon's tomb. I saw the two coffins all slewed to one side and open to view.

My job in south-east London was with a small firm headed by two Christian brothers who failed to agree, or perhaps it should be more correctly stated that the elder bullied the younger, and I found myself a go-between. It had been my ambition to have a business of my own, but after a year in the new job in which I had done rather well I was hoodwinked into being made a director. For this high post and doing any dirty work that cropped up, the emolument was an extra week's holiday a year. I had to invest some £200 in the company, money they were glad to have, especially as the new shop they had opened had not been a success. That extra week was a great boon and we were able to emulate those holidays in dear old Suffolk of my young days.

For these it was my great good fortune to find accommodation at the old city of Dunwich in the village post office, which was in the street facing the salt marshes and the sea. This was kept by an old sailor, a native who had served on the China Station, and the post office was in the downstairs front room. Just by the door was a weather glass and the post box. Every now and then he would come out to have a look through his telescope, especially if there was a ship in sight.

Mrs Darkins, our landlady, was a delightful person of the lady's maid type, as clean as a new pin and kindness itself to my wife, then a young mother. Without a word when we were out she would collect any little bits of washing she could find, they would be cleaned and ironed and put in a little pile in the bedroom. How much that niceness was appreciated cannot be expressed. Those holidays continued until she could have us no longer.

Our next holiday was to a boarding house higher up the coast, but so different that I vowed I would not have another. However, I borrowed a bicycle, went down to Westleton, the next village to that Middleton of which I have already written, to see if I could buy a cottage. Instead of one I got three for £50; one was occupied but the other two were under threat of condemnation. They were to be a godsend, the first piece of Suffolk soil I owned. I had the two done up and then called in the local authority to inspect them. An official came but still insisted they were not fit for permanent residence, yet would serve as a holiday home. They are still there and occupied.

The next thing was furnishing them, which was an easy task as far as I was concerned. The staircase in the middle cottage was not too bad, but the other was impossible and had to be almost removed to get anything up. The two cottages were kept separate and when fitted up were a joy. How the children loved it all. But sad to relate, well water did not seem to suit them, nor the milk from a neighbour's cows that was far too rich and the first few days of their holiday gave them stomach upsets. But that did not stop them from entering into village life where people belonged, with names that conjured up generations of families. Once upon a time and that not distant the village possessed three windmills, while the church, thatched like the one at Middleton, stood among the graves of those whose names were honoured. It was there the wheelwright and undertaker played the organ, while his wife kept the post office.

I had never lost my love for that part of East Suffolk and had taken up some research work on Dunwich while living in London. I managed to get a reader's ticket to the British Museum and plodded away at the State Papers. Some of my mother's people had come from Westleton and Grandmother's brother had moved there to carry on his trade as a builder. He had left his mark behind in the school with its Jubilee clock, school house, and a number of stone-built cottages.

As far as my job was concerned I managed to hold it down for nineteen years, or it held me down for that period. It is rather a curious thing to look back on those days in the light of our present time. The all-important thing was to keep the figures mounting upwards, next year must beat this, until one wondered when it would stop and how long one could keep it up. Profits were not then a dirty word or prosperity something to be shunned. True, it was apt to give one a bit of a headache but it was an interesting incentive. My personal aim then was to attain a salary of £500 a year, something that was to take a long time to achieve. All went well for a few brief years until the war clouds began to darken the sky.

I remember sitting at breakfast one morning and realizing that if the war actually came it would completely wreck our little household. I had planned our new old house to be a wonderful home for the children, thinking the extensive garden would be a veritable wonderland, but with the curious intricacies of children's minds they much preferred a room that was allotted to them as a playroom. They certainly used it as such and you never saw such a paradise of a chaotic mess in your life. But it was their very own. And then the storm broke.

The family was in our country cottage and on return our

daughter, a little girl of eight, went away with her school as a boarder to Sussex. She did not come home again until she was sixteen. Later on when visiting her I came back to find that the Battle of Britain had been fought in our skies and a woman killed in an adjoining road. Soon after that the younger boy of four went to join his sister, but my wife nearly wept when we went to see them and watched him trying to do his evening toilet by himself before bed. Soon the elder boy had gone too and we were alone.

Meanwhile the war waged on, Dunkirk had become a great memory and our locality began to fill up with soldiers, notably a regiment of Guards. Then came the blitz on London and there was not a night when something or other was dropped on Upper Norwood and we discovered we were living in Bomb Alley. It got so hot that they began to move the troops, because it was noised abroad that it was too dangerous for them. I paid a visit one Sunday afternoon to my old home and the thought passed through my mind that it was too close to the railway. The next morning my old aunt and brother were on our doorstep, having been bombed out. Aunt was then eighty-four, but that bomb put new life into her and she would persist in returning to the poor old wreck with my wife, jumping over the rubble to rescue some of her treasures. They would return with the sirens droning out their direful sounds. Eventually the house was left with its contents intact, Father's workshop just as he left it and the broken window never properly repaired since the last cricket match with the drain pipe as a wicket.

I had managed to buy up a whole library of books and had stacked them up in piles around the playroom. At that period we all slept downstairs and while aunt was with us a bomb dropped nearby and all the books fell inwards. Her only comment was, "Lawks-a-mussey, what's a matter!" She was at last persuaded to go to one of the cottages, reluctantly, where she lived for another four years.

It was now those cottages came into their own, because as

the holidays came round we used to snatch up the children and take them there. How they got to love it all, the only time they could be together. When we were finally bombed out the two boys went to the village school.

During the phoney war the two boys returned home and were with us for the bombing. When fires were started the younger would look out from his bedroom window and say, "Bromley has got it tonight." Then when the shrapnel fell the reaction was, "I bags that bit in the morning." My wife's sister, a nurse, had come home from the Lebanon. Her boat was in convoy when it was attacked by an enemy submarine. The passengers were ordered to the boats, in the excitement the ropes were cut and she was plunged into the sea where she remained for four hours. She had given up hope when a destroyer caught her in its searchlights and she was saved. She was a plucky woman and would come to us sometimes when she thought we were in for a raid.

I was doing quite a lot of writing, chiefly for trade journals and sometimes a magazine. I also wrote my first country book *Suffolk Yesterdays* and had the usual job of getting it published. In the end I paid for it (or part of it I was told). I remember the dilemma, should I part with my money or not? It seemed ages before it appeared and when it did the flying bombs were upon us. I said goodbye to my money but the book sold out before Christmas. This led to another which was not so successful.

The night bombing was pretty awful but the flying bombs were meant to strike terror and they did as far as I was concerned. To hear them coming, the drone of the engine which literally made the earth tremble and then the dreadful silence as the engine cut out was too awful for anything. The first one passed over our house to fall on Streatham where it wrecked two hundred houses. The V bombs worried me far less. We were finally put out by a flying bomb on the Sunday morning when the Guards Chapel was hit. We had ours about 5 a.m., theirs was during the morning service. By then we were on our way to Suffolk leaving it all behind for a space of quiet.

As a business we had been caught up in the spate of black-out fever. How the public scrambled and so did we. Our outside man would go up to town with his car for a load in the morning and it would be all gone by tea time. The same to-morrow and the next day. Then came Purchase Tax and the thought that one had better be careful and not buy too much lest one got caught when it should be taken off! But it made things dear. They called it a phoney war and said it would be over by Christmas, if not certainly by Easter. An article I wrote, called "Random Reflections" for a trade paper gives some idea of our problems, of which I give extracts:

1940, a few exhibitions of furniture in London but not many buyers. No famine and no rush. War not over; travellers still calling with their old wives' tales as to date of the end, but then, they assured us the war would never start. Said they knew some-one who knew Hitler, and he wasn't such a fool as that! Now—'I've got a line of gas mask cases here; we've cut up our rexine; something to keep the girls busy!' Business on a fairly level keel, but not a lot doing in carpets and furniture. Even had a trip to High Wycombe—yes, they executed the orders; but I didn't think it would be the last visit! True, they talked of orders for thousands and thousands of tent-pegs, wondering if the army were going to light their pipes with them. And some of the doors were shut.

Oh, yes, went to Kidderminster too. Driven by the representa-tive in a fast sports car, said he was waiting to get into the Air Force. Ah, come to think of it, that accounted for the pace; evidently thought he was in blue! Beastly journey back though; France had capitulated. Had a wireless on board and heard the sad, ominous voice of Duff Cooper. Potential airman said he was only interested in one battle—the last, and that not yet. Thank God, it wasn't; but soon will be.

Then there was that bit of bombing—not very pleasant. Came to business one morning and didn't have to go in by the usual door—windows on the path. Land-mine they said; however, patched them up and started again. Have to rake round and find out what happened to those wholesalers in the City. Gone up in smoke many of them; moved to another address and burnt out there. But you can't kill the wholesaler! Perfect phoenixes. Better wait awhile, they'll turn up again. Few posts later: "Owing to enemy action our address is now . . . and our telephone number is. . . ." Good old wholesalers; and what a nice little address. This desirable residence! Bombing leaves off, don't know why, and trade begins to boom and, unfortunately, prices soar, especially second-hand. No new furniture allowed to be made!

1942. Sunday morning announcement: clothes to go on coupons, and to include soft furnishings! Consternation in that section; fancy old so-and-so snipping off little bits of paper! So we have to take margarine coupons for a bit of cretonne and one's curtains are graded with the Fats! Added to this, no patterns, which is a blessing; but what is to become of the shopper who collects those things? And *no paper*! But then, old so-and-so could never make a decent parcel.

1943—Utility furniture. On view near Hanover Square; must go and see that. Meet some of the manufacturers who hang about the stands and finger the doors, and look as though a mountain had given birth to a mouse! Catalogues issued bearing Government crown, so we are on to a good thing now; no allowances for specials—take it or leave it and, they might add, Wait for it!

1944—D-day, and flying bombs, resulting in a shower of dockets. Dockets for this, dockets for that—fifteen square yards for your curtains (shades of the former years!) sheets, blankets, linoleum, mattresses. Then control of second-hand furniture, so that Mother's dressing chest and her nice little sideboard and her poor old wardrobe have all been given a cubic capacity, a number and a price too! Somehow was under the impression that Second-hand was controlled before. Must have made a mistake! Oh, yes, and that other little affair known as PAYE! Of course, how could I forget it? Didn't it make our secretary join the ranks of that hated brigade—the tax gatherers?

1945 . . . Let's hope we shan't blot it!

Curiously enough the model for a Utility dining chair was that of the traditional Suffolk chair, only with slatted seats in wood to economize. We found one cast up on Dulwich beach.

And so the war came to an end, the bells rang out and at evening the lights went up. It was then the little streets came into their own, with bonfires and a tea in the open air. I have always thought it was in the little streets that true patriotism was most marked, with flags at the windows always ready for a national occasion. I know it was so in our St Hugh's Road. Upper Norwood had its bonfire that consisted of laundry baskets of which there seemed to be stacks.

In my life I have done many a foolish and stupid thing short of the criminal. After the war, sometime in the forties, I bought a mansion in Suffolk almost accidentally, with no money in the bank. It happened this way. We discovered that the whole village of Dunwich—the one time capital city of East Anglia now buried in the tide—was to come up for sale. The owner had two estates and realized that one had to go. We wanted a cottage, something better than those we had, so I thought we would attend the sale. It should be mentioned that the estate had passed to a new owner, but was being sold again for the second time.

It seemed like a judgement day for the village; everything possible had been lotted up including the churchyard on the cliff, but through public feeling that was withdrawn. We had a look at the house we thought would suit but found it required too much, so we turned to the mansion which I remarked to my wife I wouldn't have at a gift. I even suggested we went home, but she thought not. The sale was held in a finely panelled room which had two baronial fireplaces. All the local world was there so we took our seats on a form at the back as being less than the least. I had not read the catalogue properly because with some of the lots any standing timber had to be paid for separately at valued prices. After the sale of the first three lots the new owner came into the room and announced that the timber for lot 4 was to be thrown in valued at £2,000.

So we came to lot 4 and I was anxious to see who was to be the new owner of the place. Bidding started, it got to £6,000, limped to £7,000, struggled on to £7,500 and the auctioneer was going to knock it down. I thought there was some mistake, poked up my hand and a voice rang out like some judge at a criminal trial, "It's on you, sir!", brought down his hammer and this huge affair was mine for £7,750. There was a silence that could be felt as I stood up and gave my name. What had I done? I hoped the floor would open and let me through. My wife nearly fainted and moaned, "I wish I hadn't come!"

What had I bought? A country house of many rooms, bathrooms galore, that had developed from a shooting box into a pseudo-Elizabethan manor, with a self-contained flat for a chauffeur, stabling, a laundry cottage, dairy cottage, and about 43 acres of land to say nothing of the standing timber.

But there was more than that. I think I had become the squire for my brief tenure and had the wreck of the sea on the foreshore as my lot. (Fortunately there were no wrecks during my holding.) There was a very high water-tower which I had to maintain to supply two or three cottages, worked by a ram at the end of the village where the river crossed the road. In the grounds was a cemetery for favourite horses and dogs complete with Victorian gravestones and inscriptions of affection. Also a circular, enclosed brick-built ring for a former squire to exercise his mounts whatever the weather. And a *ghost*, because soldiers billetted there had seen him on his horse. But they may have been at the local inn that exhibited the arms of the family. So I really had got a lot for the money I did not possess.

To tell the truth, I thought some reliable person would offer me a profit on the deal after the sale but there were no such offers. On the Monday we made our way home and my first visit was to the bank manager. To my surprise he greeted me with open arms, told me not to worry and that the bill would be settled. I then made for my solicitor who treated me in like manner and said his fees could wait. In fact they were both very interested in the transaction.

The next task was to get rid of it which proved none too

easy. I offered it for £9,000. One schemer said he would buy it and unknown to me had already asked about £19,000 for it. He would not sign the contract or pay the deposit. What he was after was an easy rake-off.

Alas, that property was to rest heavily on my shoulders, as well it might, for I had to hold on to it for a year. If I had occasion to visit the place I used to creep past lest it fell on me. I had no offers and the market seemed dead, but I was anxious to keep the lot intact. It had been used as a radar station, owing to the significance of its position and outlook on the famous Sole Bay. But it really was in a lovely spot, with the gardens ending in a ha-ha, beyond which was a level meadow leading to the edge of a crumbling cliff.

Eventually I sold it to a young doctor who hoped to turn it into a nursing home, for which it was eminently suitable. However, I fear his purchase bit his fingers more than it had done mine. Someone else reaped the fortune I was unable to grasp, but knew it was there.

The tale has lost its significance today because of the fall in the value of money. £7,750 was a small fortune then, now it will only buy a country cottage, one needing renovations at that.

I did not make much out of that transaction, if anything after expenses were met. On the top landing was a bookcase full of books. I took them away and still have them. They have proved to be of value. Some have lovely coloured plates hand-done by an old lady of the house. Her work can be seen in Suckling's *History of Suffolk.*

Soon after returning home I met more trouble, this time with my own home. One morning my wife rang me up to say that American soldiers were in our garden cutting down the trees. I rushed home to inform the man in charge that they were on our property. I met with surprise, as they thought it was a bit of derelict ground. Then came a nasty aggressive reply—"Well anyhow, we're taking your garden!" We were to learn of the absolute power of local magnates wielding an iron hand without the velvet glove. Apparently I had no right to complain if they had omitted to send me a notice of compulsory requisition. After being dispossessed of the whole property at their valuation we were put in a requisitioned house. I felt I never wanted another home in London and only those who were treated in like manner would understand. This was before the days of giving a fair price for property stolen by autocracy.

In the meantime I had bought a very nice house in Westleton, Suffolk, with outhouses, including an old railway carriage. This I used as a museum for bygones. It was a wonderful collection I managed to get together and a most delightful occupation seeking the old things and saving them from destruction, bringing them home in triumph. But it grew to such proportions that I had to abandon the idea. Like the camel and the tent, it would have put us into the street, so in the end it went to America to a pen-friend I had made through *Country Life*.

# 13

# Return to Suffolk

---

Called on Miss Strickland—the perfect blues: she seems to think the most fortunate thing in life is to get a name; nevertheless very interesting. She showed me letters from Guizot etc, and evidently thought herself the historian of the age.

MRS EASTLAKE

Because of my own folly I left London and my job for good. I took another executive post in Suffolk which proved abortive within two years and I was on my uppers except for a little money I had managed to save. It was a bleak outlook and I almost gave up hope. Then suddenly the scene changed and at sixty-four years of age I started all over again. I found a shop at a low rental, opened accounts with firms I knew and who knew me, and hoped for the best. It was to prove the most interesting venture of my life. I counted every penny and made sure I did not take one step that might lead into financial difficulty. My early training and experience stood me in good stead. By so doing I entered into the joy of being my own master, a very different thing to working for someone else.

East Suffolk was then recovering from the great floods of 1953 which had caused such a heavy toll of life and property. The total death roll of Felixstowe was 39, to which might be added 57 pigs, 15 cows, 1 horse, 23 rabbits, 923 fowl, 27 dogs and 32 cats.

We left our house in Westleton and bought a bungalow in old Felixstowe, just behind the parish church. I had wanted a business with accommodation above, but fortunately that was not to be, so I was able to leave it behind for meals as also to live in peace, using my bicycle which I only abandoned a few years ago, thus helping to keep myself fit. As one looks back, the changes in this small town have been phenomenal, but I am glad that I was here before urbanization got too great a hold and our part of the area was still a village; even our road was not made up. Many quiet and pleasant memories remain about those early years.

As the little business grew I found it necessary to go to town in the days of steam. It is nice to remember our once model station when the engine puffed in from Ipswich, turned round and went back again under a cloud of smoke and steam and we had to wait for another and splendid steam train, such as a Norfolkman to take us on to Liverpool Street. Those engines were almost human; but one was glad to get home again, and that it was to a Suffolk home. Now that splendid little station of ours, the pride of railway architecture, is all but derelict.

I had become a member of the C. of E. when my family was quite young. Without seeking it I found office as a church-warden, happily almost the last under the old vestry system, to serve an old Suffolk church for seven years. This church, with its truncated tower of old red brick and septaria, the latter dredged from the nearby sea-bed, is also a memorial to the Napoleonic era, since the tower was probably lowered lest it became a landmark. Then too, it has been in association with Landguard Fort, and one of its mural tablets tells a story. It is just inside the south door and reads: "In this Chancel lye interred the Remains of Adam Wood Esq., of the Independent Company of Invalides at Landguard Fort, who died 3rd January 1822 aged 85. This Tablet is erected as a mark of filial affection by Sir George Adam Wood, K.C.B. and K.H.T." Now Sir George had entire command of the Artillery at Waterloo.

An interesting and typical Victorian memorial is in the churchyard. It is to Sir Spencer Login who was surgeon to the residency, Lucknow during the Mutiny, and was given charge of the youthful Maharajah Dhuleep Singh (1833–93), together with the Koh-i-noor diamond. The Maharajah had the memorial erected and Queen Victoria chose the text.

I hardly thought I should live to see the Authorized Version of the Old Book supplanted by the New English Bible with its naïve language, so that modern youth can understand what they read. I can't help thinking the excuse is its own accusation. One of the most damning remarks made by a highly placed cleric was that modern compilers would not be able to mutilate the Collects. And as for Series Three, no thank you! Is there not something to be said for following in the way our forbears have trod?

Within the first five years of opening the business I said to my wife one day that we would go on holiday to Spain when package tours first began. Her excitement exceeded mine. We flew from Blackbushe near Eversley and I remember asking her if we were off the ground yet. In those early days of unpressurized planes there was a certain amount of air sickness as there had been train sickness when I was a boy. As we passed over the Pyrenees we were having a meal and I thought of my old grandfather and what he would have made of it, when the thought of a train journey from Suffolk to London made him feel ill. I also thought the stark sable-looking mountain range would have been a nasty place on which to make a forced landing; and so we came to Zaragoza. There a coach was waiting to take us the long hot dusty journey to Madrid.

All roads lead to Madrid as all the milestones measure from there. Two memories stand out: one is the Royal Palace—we had seen nothing so regal until we went to Russia; and the other was the Prado.

Toledo left an abiding memory with its narrow streets, its bridge across the Tagus, its Moorish atmosphere and not least a sunset enjoyed from the opposite bank. It was as though the ancient world was sinking into a golden memory; antiquity was in every stone. But what shall one say of that gorgeous Cathedral, seat of the Archbishop Primate of Spain? Its vastness and splendour are only outdone by Burgos. Then we were taken to El Greco's house and wandered through the rooms where that great artist lived and worked.

We travelled on to Córdoba, the Mecca of the West. There the great sight is the Cathedral which was once a mosque and one of the largest in the world at that. Neither did we miss the bridge with sixteen arches across the Guadalquivir. Seville was a slight disappointment to me because it was so crowded. However, if the cathedral contained more than I could absorb, it held something before which I stood with awe and reverence, the tomb of Christopher Columbus; the one intrepid sailor who discovered the New World. Queen Isabella, who made possible the journey, must have been a remarkable woman.

Algeciras was our next call from which we crossed to Tangier, making the return crossing on a luminous morning to Gibraltar. The view of the Rock standing out from the blue waters remains in the memory, it was once the stepping stone to India. We did not miss the monkeys. How I laughed as I watched a grandfather ape endeavouring to squeeze through a coach door while a fragile woman was making a frantic exit through another. They all but mobbed my wife when they found she had some biscuits.

Entering Spain once more we made for Málaga and thence to Granada with its palace of the Alhambra and the garden. If it is but a fragment of its former self what must it have been like in the days of its splendour? I was also interested that Washington Irving's *Tales of the Alhambra* was still on sale, particularly as I had a first edition. Then on to Valencia and Zaragoza heading for home. This was to be the first of our many holidays abroad together.

I have been able to pursue my supplementary career as a writer, a calling which has given me the greatest satisfaction. I know of nothing else to equal it for a worth-while occupation, but alas it would have been a poor living (*vide* Charles Lamb's advice to the Woodbridge poet, Bernard Barton). Most of my books and articles have been of Suffolk and its country life of yesterday, also I have pursued local history which is a rather fascinating study. I can truthfully say I have derived quite as much pleasure from this work as any I may have given.

So my wife and I have been able to do some very interesting foreign travel, visiting Egypt, the Holy Land and Petra, Russia, United States and Canada, Turkey, Bulgaria, Eastern Europe and Czechoslovakia, Greece and India, Italy and Portugal; including the Algarve which we got to love so much. I have already written of the first visit to Spain so I will end with India, fulfilling a boyhood ambition, since I was born in a half-pay district for old soldiers of the Queen and members of the Indian Civil. It recalled a scene of my boyhood when my mother took me to see the funeral of an old Mutiny veteran, Major-General Sir William Olpherts, V.C. who ended his days in our Anerley. It was a memorable occasion to watch the coffin draped with the Union Jack being carried away by a detachment of the Royal Artillery.

But where does one start with India? The answer is Delhi, Old and New, the capital, once the scene of the famous Durbars, as also the Mutiny.

Our first visit was to the Red Fort, once the headquarters of the British Raj and still used by the Indian Army. This was also the home of the Indian princes of fabulous wealth and the Peacock Throne now in Persia. Naturally we were taken to see the sacred spots between the Old and the New Delhi on the right bank of the Yamuna where Ghandi was cremated; we also passed the funeral pyre of Nehru. Our tour included modern Delhi finely laid out with Parliament buildings and offices bearing names such as Connaught Place to remind us that the fine old Duke spent some years here.

The next day we made for Agra which is surely the Englishman's idea of India. If it is possible to concentrate the beauties of a sub-continent in one building it is the Taj Mahal. It was built by Shah Jahan as an expression of his great love for his beautiful consort Mumtaz Mahal. She had died at the age of thirty-eight at the birth of her fourteenth child. It backs on to the Yamuna so that no other building can take away from its exquisite setting. The marble panels within have mellowed to an ivory shade, and carnations and tulips stand out in high relief. The two tombs are decorated with inlaid work of flowers, notably poppies on that of the Queen. They are lustrous with onyx, jasper, cornelian, jade, agate and lapis lazuli, the latter from Persia. Nearby is the Pearl Mosque built by Shah Jahan of pure white marble, voted by Nehru as one of the gems of India.

And so we came to Jaipur, to a hotel that was once the Palace of the Maharajah. The rooms were palatial but Victorian in furnishings. The grounds were so green and beautiful that we might have been in England. Our first sight was the Palace of the Winds, a towering façade of many tiers and windows but of no depth. Then on to the deserted town and Palace of Amber which left me bereft of adjectives. Its lustrous walls and coved ceilings glowed with mirror inlay work of silvered glass. Afterwards we were to see the City Palace and in one of its courtyards that had four gates—Peacock, Lotus, Sun God and Emperor—our Queen was once received.

We had to get up early for our next flight to Udaipur. Our hotel was to be the Palace of the Lake, fantastically beautiful in every detail. The courtyards, flowers and marble walls were quite out of this world. It is described as the Venice of India. A domed roof was topped by an amber pinnacle that shone in the sun, nearby was a domed oriel and in the midst a glass fountain. While here we were taken to see a Hindu Temple, an extraordinary building that rose tier on tier of white marble, carved with fantastic scenes, dancing girls predominating. So we passed to Bombay to see the Gate of India and stay at the Taj Mahal.

Next came the Ellora caves and whilst I was there I managed to visit an old English cemetery mostly graves of soldiers. Then came the rock-hewn Temple of Kailan which is considered one of the wonders of the world.

Our journey home was on a faulty plane which meant many forced landings until finally it had to be abandoned and we made the remainder of the journey by Air India by which we had set out.

*Envoi*
And when life's sweet fable ends,
Soul and body part like friends;
No quarrels, murmurs, no delay;
A kiss, a sigh, and so away.
RICHARD CRASHAW

# Postscript

There is a Latin phrase that has been in the mouths of men since the days when Horace wrote it— *laudator temporis acti.* It described a testy grumbler inclined to praise the way the world went when he was a boy. But Horace said more than that: "The tide of years as it rises brings many conveniences, as it ebbs carries many away."

The morning of youth was not always sunshine although we are apt to think it was, our Queen Victoria had been on the throne for sixty years, and those long years had brought about a sense of security, even finality. Surely our great statesmen were far too wise to wage exterminating wars, yet it was Festus who said to St Paul—"much learning doth make thee mad". The Prince Consort talked of the Great Exhibition of 1851 as showing through the works of industry of all nations, the progress of the human race. Wisdom was coming into its own, he said. The days were coming to pass when swords would be beaten into ploughshares, spears into pruning hooks, nation should not lift up sword against nation, neither shall they learn war anymore. Then, after a long widowhood the old Queen died and the nation was fearful as the funeral train, with blinds drawn, wended its way to Windsor.

I can recall that feeling of finality. Some time ago I picked up the tattered remains of an old directory of my native bit of London. That too seemed to have reached its prime, but in turning over the pages I was astonished at the number of empty houses. There were scores. Then came the War, when even Christian ministers eulogized the slaughter of others, so that our population was to fall leaving more room for those who survived. However, by an incredible miracle things did not happen that way and soon, so very soon there was a housing shortage.

There was another significant feature about the days of our youth and that was that they were never long enough. A working day was of as many hours as employers could make it, and there was talk of wasting time. It is hardly necessary to point out the moral or mark the swing of the pendulum. But there was one thing vouchsafed to youth which is not granted to age, the joy and speculation of looking forward. What would one do or be? The striving after, even if it ended in failure. Surely it were better to have loved and lost than never to have loved at all.

Short commons and penury brought a compensating appreciation of things and advantages bestowed. I remember lining up in our playground at school when we were dismissed for a whole month's holiday in the summer. What a slice of time that seemed to be.

Although the tide of years has brought many conveniences, more money, goods, opportunities, even luxury; yet the ebb has carried away appreciation, independence, satisfaction, peace. The throb of the engine is for ever in our ears, so that our very existence depends on oil and the pace is faster than sound. The anomaly exists that our scientists are extending the number of our days and seeking also to find the means of extinguishing us altogether. To many, surely, the great loss of all is that of morals, honesty and discipline.

Why, then, this cult of the so-called antique, even to the extent of an old fender and fire-irons, especially if they happen to resemble those on view at the Great Exhibition? Or the cult of reproduction furniture, especially old oak, now made somewhere in Europe and snapped up faster than produced? Is it an unconscious groping after something we have lost? Something which the jet age or the permissive society cannot give?

Surely it is a looking backward to certainty and peace, the age of innocence. After all, the flowers in our little bit of gardens, so assiduously cultivated had not lost their smell as those richer and finer blooms appear to have done today.

> Som tyme this world was so steadfast and stable
> That mannes word was obligacioun,
> And now hit is so fals and deceivable,
> That word and deed, as in conclusioun,
> Ben no-thing lyk, for turned up so doun
> Is al this world for mede and wilfulnesses,
> That al is lost for lak of steadfastness.
>
> GEOFFREY CHAUCER